THE CHILD JESUS

THE CHILD JESUS

ADEY HORTON

The Dial Press/New York/1975

*à Vincent
et à ses parents*

First Dial printing, 1975

Designed and produced by Walter Parrish International Limited, London

Designed by Judy A. Tuke

ISBN 0-8037-5379-9

Library of Congress Catalog Card No: 75-11922

Printed and bound in Spain by Roner S.A., Madrid
Dep. Legal: SS. 356-1975

title page illustration
1 The Flight from Bethlehem. Detail from the Buxtehude Altar, Hamburg, painted on
wood by Master Bertram in the late fourteenth century.

Contents

To help the reader see how points in the text are illustrated in the pictures, in the text margin are the numbers of illustrations where they are specially relevant.

2 Mary is knitting the garment without a seam for which the soldiers beneath the cross cast lots (John, xix, 23). Jesus has been reading and playing with his top; but already the angels are holding symbols of his Passion. A second detail from the Buxtehude altar, Hamburg, late fourteenth century.

Colour Illustrations

3 The Annunciation to Mary: framed in the far window, a tiny Jesus, on his way to Mary's ear, is descending the celestial beam. By the 'Master E–S', *c.* 1500.

Introduction

Today, we know little of the circumstances of the life of Mary and nothing of the early years of her son, save that he was carried into Egypt and returned from there to Nazareth and that once, when he was twelve years old, he escaped from his family and returned to the Temple of Jerusalem where he astonished the Doctors with his precocity. Yet five hundred years ago, which is but one quarter of the Christian span, the people of all the Christian lands still knew a great deal about Mary's life and about the lives of her parents and family and a great deal of the birth and childhood and youth of her firstborn son, Jesus. What they knew they did not know from books, for few could read. But in an illiterate world scores of tales of the mother and her child had been handed down from the earliest times from generation to generation by word of mouth, handed down within so strong a framework of memory and sustained belief that the same stories were known not only throughout the Orthodox East, which was nearer to its subject, but, with some modifications for local colour, throughout the West. Many of these stories were as old as the canon, the authorised Scriptures which we know, and had their origins among those same Levantine peoples who saw the emergence of the Gospels. Some, we believe, were of later origin, though still of ancient date, and some may have been the inventions of pious thought. But for very many centuries they coloured the beliefs, and so the lives, of Christian men; and for a millennium, from early in our era to the full flood of the Renaissance, artifacts of every kind, in depicting them, performed their function of reminding mankind of ancient truths: artifacts which today we cannot properly understand or appreciate unless we know these stories themselves. It is the purpose of this book to examine these stories, the biblical and un-biblical alike, and to relate them to the artifacts which illustrate them, some of which are among the greatest works of men's hands.

4 The Adoration of the Kings—in the first half of the fourteenth century, there is not yet a black monarch. Attributed to Andrea Orcagna (*c.* 1308–*c.* 1368).

Today, all this material is quite, or almost quite forgotten. Today, few laymen, and even few clerics, read the New Testament with critical attention or remember precisely what they read. Moreover we tend to imagine that everything we ourselves know, or that we could know of the lives of Mary and her child comes from the texts of the four Evangelists Matthew, Mark, Luke and John. It is fortunate that this is not the case, for even a cursory examination of the Gospels shows us that Mark and John do not even record the birth of Jesus and that John, indeed, seems not even to have known the name of his mother. Matthew and Luke have more to say about the matter. But if we compare the accounts which they give of the birth and the earliest days of Jesus we find ourselves confronted with two narratives which are not only quite distinct in manner and feeling but which in matter, in the tale they tell, are so different from one another and in many respects so contradictory that it is difficult to believe that they are recording the same birth to the same mother of the same child.

Our own ideas of what actually happened in that winter in Palestine some two thousand years ago are made up of a fusion of the two accounts, to which we add remembered fragments of the far more detailed version of them which once existed; backed up in the mind's eye by the vast number of pictures which show us such scenes as the Birth, or the Flight into Egypt. Our scenario is relatively simple: most of us remember and recognise the Annunciation of the Angel, and the visit of the pregnant Mary to the pregnant Elisabeth. Everyone who has ever been to a picture gallery has a reasonably clear idea of the birth itself, with the child in the manger, or on his virgin mother's knee, with the shepherds before them and Joseph detached a little to one side: all of which illustrates Luke's story. Then there are the Wise Men, usually dressed up as the Three Kings who are so familiar to us: whose own story leads us beyond the birth to Herod and the Massacre of the Innocents and the Flight of the Holy Family to Egypt, a tale so marvellous and so sanguinary that it is disconcerting to find that only Matthew mentions it.

The two stories are mixed in the minds of all of us; and as we should expect, the Christmas cribs of churches of every denomination, which are our only current and regular representations of the tale, bring the two together quite unhesitatingly. And not only do they do this, but they expand the biblical stories and introduce characters and incidents which we accept without question, but which in fact have nothing to do with what Matthew and Luke actually recorded in either of their disparate accounts. In the New Testament there is no ox, nor any ass to warm the swaddling infant with its breath on that cold December night; and no stable to house them, or their masters. There is

5 The Massacre of the Innocents in a mural at Assisi. By Giotto, *c.* 1290.

6 This papyrus fragment, dating from about A.D. 150 and containing a few verses from St John's Gospel, is the oldest copy of any portion of the New Testament known to be in existence today.

no mention at all of those Three Kings whom we know so well, and even the Shepherds do not 'adore' the child. Moreover, in the cribs of the more ambitious churches and in so many of the pictures not only of the Birth but of all the other happenings of the early life of Jesus we find other things going on and other figures crowding the scene, none of whom have any place in the Bible. What, we might ask, is this all about? Where do these people come from and what are they doing here?

The response to these questions is exceedingly complex. To begin to answer them, we must sketch in briefly the background of the Gospels, and the early history of the church. Firstly, we do not really know who Matthew, Mark, Luke and John were. None of them could have known Jesus: and the question of when they lived and when the Gospels which bear their names were first committed to writing is one which has for centuries sustained an impassioned and sometimes furious debate. One of the four books may have been composed in Rome, but the origins of the others are generally ascribed to widely separated areas of the ancient Levantine world; and the earliest surviving manuscripts which contain any accounts of the virgin birth or of the childhood of Jesus date from at least two centuries after the events which they record. The writings which we know come, then, not from the Jewish and monotheistic world which Jesus knew but from primitive Christian communities of a later time, each of which would have had a related but by no means identical version of the Christian story as it had been handed down to them through a number of generations: sometimes, perhaps, by word of mouth alone. Matthew for example, might have worked in Greece, Luke, perhaps, in Egypt, and at a different time. Each area had its own traditions and each, perhaps, its own needs; and under these circumstances the radical differences between the biblical versions of the stories which chiefly concern us, though they make for poor history, are understandable.

Furthermore, in the first centuries of our era the fledgling Christian communities differed widely among themselves on major points of doctrine, and most schools of thought supported their views in weighty theological writings. The Gospels of the four Evangelists, probably in a form very close to that in which we know them, were accepted at a quite early date—certainly by the year 200—as primary sources for the life of Jesus; but these works did not by any means stand alone as histories and interpretations of the Christian message, nor did their authority go unchallenged. For centuries, a 'New Testament' in the sense of a generally agreed corpus of writings forming a canon of divine inspiration, did not exist, the primacy of a Pope at Rome—for there were others—was not by any means established, and no central source of unquestioned authority directed the thoughts and attitudes of the church. Christianity, which was more than once proscribed in the Roman Empire as a subversive sect, did not spring from the earth fully armed with an accepted doctrine and establishment, but pieced itself together with infinite labour in a volatile Levantine world where polemic was an end in itself, an enjoyable and popularly appreciated exercise. Specific Christian doctrines such as that of the Trinity, or of the true nature of Christ, were subtle, complex and elusive: heaven-sent matters for debate. In the intellectual climate of the area and time, not only competing doctrines but even delicate shades of theological meaning were upheld by their respective adherents with such dramatic intensity that more than once the Church was split asunder. No other world religion, at its beginnings, has had so heavy a cross to bear.

Nevertheless, the infant church grew fast: perhaps even faster, in those early centuries, than its great rival Mithraism. And it had a geographical advantage over competing faiths, for its power centres were strung along the African seaboard and lay thickly in those eastern Mediterranean provinces—Egypt, and Syria, and Asia Minor—whence Rome drew the greatest part of her wealth, her luxuries and even her strength. The weight of Empire lay not in the primitive and turbulent West, but there in the East in her richest lands set towards the borders of Persia, the only competing civilised power: and when, early in the fourth century Constantine the Great actually shifted his capital city from Rome to the East, to the new Rome of Constantinople, and embraced this eastern faith of Christianity as the official religion of the Empire, it was time for the lusty young church to set its house in order once and for all.

The official church, quite clearly, must have its official doctrine. Among the competing theological factions, the battle for supremacy was long and bitter, though not particularly bloody. Power changed hands a number of times, but it was rare that a dissenter from the views currently prevailing earned more than anathema and banishment. And by about the end of this fourth century the central struggle was over and the adherents of one specific theological system emerged as victors and established the doctrinal framework of the Catholic and Universal Church in that basic form in which it is maintained today in the church of Rome, and which finds its reflection in the Thirty-Nine Articles of the Church of England and in the tenets of the Episcopal Church of America.

Other views, naturally, were still held by many, and a lively tradition of a certain, if limited freedom of expression had grown up within the faith. But with a specific body of doctrine established by an official ruling body, dissent from it became by definition heresy, and dissenting writings, heretical writings. Heretics could be dealt with, and were dealt with with increasing rigour; but it was necessary to specify for all the faithful what could, and what could not be read. After much residual argument within the new Establishment, the major part of the canon, or accepted books of the New Testament, was fixed once and for all, and the unaccepted theological and 'Apocryphal' writings were rejected once and for all by the Gelasian Decree 'De Libris Recipiendis et non Recipiendis' which, disconcertingly for so famous a document, can only be dated as 'Gallic ?Vth C'. Formulated at a time when doctrinal passion still smouldered it was, as it had to be, a quite

opposite
7 St Jerome at work in his study on the 'Vulgate' Bible pauses to remove the thorn from the lion's paw: an act more properly attributed to St Geronimus. Jerome's Latin version of the scriptures (*c.* 400) was the first authoritative recension of the earlier texts current at that time. The painting is part of an altarpiece by Antonio Niccolo Colantonio, active 1440–70.

overleaf
8 The 'Annunciation' to Joachim that his wife will give birth to Mary. Stained-glass window at Chalons-sur-Marne, France, sixteenth century.

uncompromising document, and it concluded its list of rejections with a ringing sentence of Proustian complexity of which the last phrase alone declares that:

> . . . Peter and the other Peter, of whom the one besmirched Alexandria and the other Antioch, Acacius of Constantinople and his associates, and what also all disciples of heresy and of the heretics and the schismatics—whose names we have scarcely deigned to preserve—have taught or compiled, we acknowledge is to be not merely rejected but excluded from the whole Roman Catholic and Apostolic Church and with its authors and the adherents of its authors to be damned in the inextricable shackles of anathema for EVER.

Disapprobation can scarcely be made more clear. And a form of dogmatic success was achieved insofar as the dissenting theological writings never recovered from the branding, and in most of the Imperial lands were destroyed with such vigour that the greater part of this material is lost to us today. We can hardly regret it. It had served its time and when, a millennium later, dissent racked the church once more and led eventually to schism, it was moved by other forces, and knew no more these ancient quarrels.

With the wholesale disappearance of those early writings which had been declared heretical, only the recently accepted books of the Bible and the works of approved theologians, together, perhaps, with border-line cases such as Tertullian, should in theory have survived. But this did not quite happen, for there were a number of anathematised texts which showed an obstinate vitality and which are still with us today, commonly grouped together as the 'Apocrypha of the New Testament'. Here we find theological and narrative works which by chance escaped Gelasius' Decree: additional 'Ministry' Gospels and fragments of Gospels, Acts, apocalyptic writings, together with Gnostic tracts, and others which are even further from the mainstream

overleaf
9 The birth of Jesus, with Salome and Maia the midwife. Bottom left: the Devil pours poisoned words into Joseph's ear, reminding him of his earlier doubts about the paternity of the child. Fifteenth-century mural in the Latin chapel in the monastery church of St John Lampadistis at Kalopanayiotis, Cyprus.

opposite
10 In this remarkable statue the mystic body of Mary conceals within itself not only her son, but all the basic elements of the Christian story. Ivory figure in the cathedral treasury at Evora, Portugal, thirteenth century.

11 Three of the four generations: St Anne enthroned, with Mary in her lap, while Mary in turn holds Jesus. From a Bohemian manuscript, fourteenth century.

of Christian thought. The survival of this particular and quite disparate group of theological and mystical texts is accidental and due to combinations of fortuitous circumstances. On the other hand, the 'Apocryphal' list includes a number of anathematised texts from which the establishment was never quite able to separate itself through the centuries, and which we know today as the 'Infancy Gospels'. It is these which primarily concern us here.

They take us into another world. These essentially simple and wonder-studded narratives tell us—and they tell us with a wealth of detail—of the family and the birth and the early years of Jesus, and of the life of his mother: filling in precisely those areas in which the brief

New Testament accounts are so sparing. Once upon a time, in a more primitive world, this information was a requirement; if it had not already existed, it would have had to have been invented. In what are called with a decent measure of truth the 'ages of faith', so many simple people, living out lives of brutish poverty and deprivation, called on Mary and her child—but particularly Mary—seeing in them elevated but recognisable beings who did not wish them ill and who might one day bring them to peace and rest and shelter. They loved them, just as in our own times the black-clothed peasant women of Sicily or Crete call on them in person, as it were, and love them still. All good came from them, all evil from elsewhere: 'I prayed to Mary, and she told her son. And so it came out alright and I got back my cow'. This was the religion of the humble, and to them, Mary and Jesus were there, immediate, understandable, and living not far away but somewhere above the church tower among the stars. Once, for a wonder, they had lived upon earth, poor people, working for their bread and sheltering in the stable when there was no room at the inn.

Mediaeval man was passionately interested in every detail of their lives, and most of all in these happenings of the time when the Mary of grace and peace had been with her little child, an innocent and uncomplicated saviour. And indeed they knew a great deal about them. That what they 'knew' came from the apocryphals did not concern them, for they knew no books. But it was from these Infancy Gospels that came the stories that all men knew, and which gave Mary loving parents and a special childhood, which told men how and in what way her son was born, which filled their journey to Egypt with magical events, and which set the child not only to work marvels in his boyhood and to know more letters than the dominies of Egypt could ever know, but to laugh and spin tops and puddle in the mud of the streams. They could understand and believe in a Mary who spun her wool and a Joseph the Carpenter who plied his trade, and a Jesus who played as other children played, and who yet worked marvels. These were stories for simple men. The Body and Blood of Christ, when they could partake of them perhaps once a year at some high festival, was a great and awesome wonder. But to hear of the joys and perils of the little family in Bethlehem, and Egypt, and Nazareth was to love them, to admire them, and through them to be led, not to an ecstatic, an elegant Paradise, but to an imaginable Heaven where there was food every day, and no winds blew.

They may have been unlettered, credulous people. But the stories which they had in their minds came from sources which were better than they knew, and to which we ourselves should pay heed today. We have seen that the Evangile is known to us in a comparatively late form, and from texts which are separated from the events which they record by at least as great a space of time as that which separates us from, say, the world of Dr Johnson, or of the American War of Independence. These are part of the ancient canon, read in church, accepted with unquestioned credence. Yet we have a complete text of one of the apocryphals, the 'Gospel of James', called the 'Protevangelium', which probably antedates and is at least contemporary with the earliest known text of any of the Evangiles. It originates from the same general area as the Gospels of the canon, and where the narrative of James overlaps with them it is clearly fed from similar traditions. Its special characteristic is that with an undoubted antiquity of authorship it unites an exceptional wealth of material which expands that story of the mother, and of the first days of Jesus, which two of the Evangelists treat somewhat summarily and according to their lights, and which two chose to ignore altogether: unless, indeed, the tale of the Virgin Mother had never reached their ears. The Protevangelium may not have the sanction of the Church, but we cannot ignore it. Our chapters 1 to 6 are based on it; and we cannot but be thankful that a venerable text of the work has survived into our own day.

Other apocryphals, in the form in which we know them, have a less certain accreditation. The 'Gospel of Thomas' was known in a Greek original to Irenaeus, who died in the year 200; and the so-called 'Pseudo-Matthew' was certainly known in the fourth, and probably in the third century. We draw extensively from both of them in the most

12 A family portrait: St Anne—the central figure—and Mary, together with their family and kin, shown in a tapestry.

ancient form in which they have come down to us. Then there is a curious document, the ' "Arabic" Gospel of the Infancy,' of which the earliest known form is an eleventh or twelfth-century Arabic translation or adaptation, of a much earlier Christian text of Syriac or Egyptian origin. It sets out the broad lines of the story as we know it from senior texts, but overlays it with an embroidery of eastern magic. This, and other less venerable writings to which we shall refer from time to time, owe a little too much to the world of the Arabian Nights: a world of wish-fulfilment to which all the apocryphals, even the Protevangelium—and even the Gospels themselves—owe something. But the debt is one of degree. In the oldest and solidest apocryphals, and in many of their passages, it is not hard for us to hear the echoes of sound tradition and the tread of ancient feet.

As we have said, the stories of the Protevangelium, and Thomas, and Pseudo-Matthew—and perhaps of many more now lost to us—were passed down from the earliest times from generation to generation by word of mouth; though here and there texts now unknown to us may have survived and helped to keep the stories in something approaching their original form. In the early days of Gelasian fervour, the church would have denied them on principle even though, as we shall see, the apocryphals do not in any way deny the gifts or the faculties or the divinity of the central figures of the Christian pantheon. We should consider the opposite to be true, for they extend the list of their interventions, and in fact they create the character of Mary *de toutes pièces*. But these writings, in many of their aspects, tend to de-mystify and to humanise them. The church, on this account alone, could not love these works: which were moreover uncanonical, often heretical, and anathematised by definition. Nevertheless, their stories were ineradicable from the minds of men; they pointed, sometimes, valuable lessons; they were, sometimes, useful; and they were not uncongenial to the mass of the clergy. So before very long had passed, the church began to use them. Some of the earliest Christian artifacts of Byzantium show apocryphal scenes, and even in the tardy Roman lands, and even as early as the ninth century, Pope Leo II himself had the story of Mary's mother and father painted on the walls of the church of St Paul in Rome. From that moment, perhaps, the Apocrypha had won its place and could begin to come into its own again in the Christian world of the West.

From about the beginning of the twelfth century, acceptance became total and with the blessing of the church actual collections of apocryphal tales, some of them original, some of them later inventions and additions mixed up with more strictly biblical matter, poured from the scriptoria of the monasteries, enriching the whole world of the later mediaeval centuries. We cannot insist too much on the fact that Christianity, basically an arcane eastern religion with elevated and astonishing mysteries, was made up in its pure form of too mystical a group of concepts for the common man—and for most of his betters—in the laborious and unphilosophic West. But in mediaeval times the Apocrypha was there and the matter of the Apocrypha softened and rounded the outlines of the Christian faith—particularly in all that surrounded the birth of Jesus—and by making some elements of Christianity more comprehensible, more digestible to the masses it rendered an incalculable service to the mediaeval church. And it continued to do so until the great upheavals of the sixteenth century, when the Roman church rejected these uncanonical stories as unworthy of the firmer discipline of the Counter-Reformation, and Protestantism banished them as Popish fables unknown to Holy Writ. Today, we have altogether forgotten them. But they were long in dying, these ancient tales, as we shall see.

The pictures

The artifacts reproduced in this book range in date and place from seventh-century Byzantium to the High Renaissance in the West, with occasional excursions beyond these limits to illustrate a particular point. The bulk of the paintings shown were executed between, say, 1300, when the painter in the West began to achieve sufficient mastery over his materials to be able to illustrate selective detail, and the first half of the sixteenth century, when the Reformation and the Counter-Reformation, in the interest of their respective theologies, drove from the scene the apocryphal subjects which chiefly concern us here. It is this large group which we hope will be looked at with particular attention, and which we would indeed ask the reader to look at in a way which may be unfamiliar: today, when we are confronted with any post-Renaissance work of art, we tend to be obnubilated by 'aesthetics', a quite modern word and a quite modern conception which is essentially concerned with the critical, the intellectual and the emotional impression which an artifact makes on the beholder. A picture, including all modern pictures, is deemed to be beautiful, or structural, or satisfying, or what you will; or it is not, and does not 'say' anything to us in the particular language of aesthetics.

The same criteria are generally applied, perhaps unthinkingly, to mediaeval paintings. But when we do this we get our priorities wrong and put, as it were, the cart before the horse. The purpose of mediaeval art was didactic. A picture told a story. An artifact was never

13 Jesus and Joseph fencing their orchard and vinery. Engraving by Hieronymous Wiercx, late sixteenth century.

created as an intellectual exercise, or as an exposé of the artist's creativity and talent, or as a demonstration of colour and composition. This is by no means to say that mediaeval man was insensitive to technical excellence. A particularly brilliant painting, a grand carving, and especially a scene captured with unusual verisimilitude, might be carried through the streets to the shouts of applause of the townspeople and the greater credit of the master man and his atelier who had created it. In those days the painter worked to rule, and the mediaeval painter was an artisan. He was a tradesman who worked to order and his standing in the world was that of any other artisan. If he was invited to his patron's table, he sat below the salt. In Italy, as likely as not, he belonged to the saddlers' guild, for there is power in numbers and there were far more saddlers — who painted their saddles — than there were painters who worked on tempera or board or canvas. They were, as a general rule, less well-to-do than for example armourers or their saddle-making colleagues, whose jobs brought them into more direct and constant contact with the knightly classes. In the early fourteenth century it had been a matter for comment that Giotto owned a substantial vineyard, and even a few looms which he hired out to his weaver neighbours; and it is not before the High Renaissance and the days of Michelangelo and Raphael that we find artisans becoming 'artists' who not only became relatively rich from their work, but who could exercise real influence on the subjects and the treatment of subjects which they executed.

The artist worked to the best of his powers and to a book of rules. In the West, his rules were less absolutely constricting than those of the Byzantine and Slavic lands, which had their own justification; but they laid down for him the overall form which he should adopt in delineating a given subject and, of course, the attributes which should be given to a particular personage, and the cast of countenance. These were what might be called the strategic rules, which imbued every picture with a symbolism which it is not the purpose of this book to explore; and any significant divagation from them was a form of heresy. Then there were the tactical rules, such as the provision of ample wavy hair to St George in order to distinguish him from the balder St Demetrius, that other warrior saint who rode his white horse in the battles of Christendom. Fortunately, such distinctions were very widely recognised and men knew what pictures and their ancillary details were about by looking at them. Few, very few, could have read a phylactery or a picture label, even if labels had been thought of at the time.

Mediaeval art represented the world's, and not the artist's pre-occupations. The artist-craftsman, who ideally started his apprentice-ship when seven years old, and who spent seven years in running errands and grinding colours and seven more as a preparer and eventually a background man, brought his carefully acquired skills to the execution of a given task which was demanded of him. It was the patron, or the 'donor' — for want of a better expression — who bespoke and paid for his work; and the patron who called the tune. For a new house or a new church suitable pictures of the required subject and size and colour mix would be ordered from a master painter in the same way as hangings would be ordered from the mercer, or the master mason instructed in the form he was to give to a chimney piece or a rood screen. Each picture might be an evocation of family history. Far more often it was a reminder, on traditional and immediately recognisable lines, of a sacred theme which was intended to bring thoughts of a sacred nature to a family or, for example, to the Regulars of a monastery who would see the picture on every day of their lives.

The themes of religious pictures were by no means necessarily from the Bible. Men did not know the Bible: they knew a Christian story which had been built up in the collective consciousness over the centuries and which owed its constituent parts to many different lands and to many different times. The edifying lives of the Saints had their place; an important place, but a place apart. In the central Christian story, or at least in that part of it which concerns us here, the matter of the Apocrypha is the mainstay of pictorial narration. That it presents material which is almost unknown to us today, and which is sometimes decried, is immaterial: this is how men once thought that great events had happened and this is how men liked their pictures to be: pictures which told a familiar story after a familiar fashion. We know them today and admire them wholeheartedly for their beauty, their serenity or their pictorial effect: but in a deeply Christian and almost wholly illiterate age they were the posters and the guide books — the mnemonics — of the time; and the purpose of each one was to remind men of a facet of the intricate Christian story and to invite them to reflection and prayer and repentance.

1 The grandparents of Jesus

In Judea, some ten years before the Emperor Augustus confirmed Herod the Great as the ruler of the province, apocryphal texts tell us that Joachim, a man of resolute piety, and rich in the possession of vast flocks and herds which pastured in the hill country of Jericho, married Anne, whose family held great estates in the north towards Mount Carmel, on the Pheonician seaboard of Galilee. They lived in Jerusalem, and were exemplary in their observance of the rituals of domestic piety and in the regularity of their attendance at the ceremonies of the Temple, to whose priests and their sacrificial table Joachim brought splendid offerings. Their wealth was such that they were able to give a third of their revenues to religious charity and a third to the Temple itself, and yet to live largely and munificently—for no begger ever knocked on their door in vain—on the remainder.

They were the grandparents of Jesus. No one, in that generation of mankind, would have imagined so sublime a destiny; least of all, perhaps, Joachim and Anne, the felicity of whose lives was marred by a single circumstance: they were childless, and at the time of our story they had been childless for twenty years. This was not only a private grief, but a public calamity, for in the Jewish theology of the time childlessness was considered to be a sign of the displeasure of God, and a barren couple, whatever the appearance of sanctity in their lives, not only lost the consideration of their church and of society but could eventually be anathematised and forbidden attendance at the ceremonies of the Temple. At these ceremonies, and particularly at the great 'Feasts of Offerings', Joachim's contributions were always twofold, and for years, in virtue of the consideration which was due to him, he was permitted to stand first among his peers and to present his offerings as he had always done. But the day came when the council of the church decided that his childlessness could no longer be overlooked; and at the next great festival, when all the people were gathered in the Temple, he found his passage to the altar barred by the High Priest Reuben in person. 'It is not fitting for you to offer your gifts,' he said, 'for you have raised up no offspring in Israel.' And Joachim, the rich and proud and pious man, was thrust from the house of Jehovah.

This was catastrophe, excommunication. The Temple was the heart and centre of the Jewish life of Jerusalem, and to be banished from it meant, for a man in Joachim's position, a traumatic loss in status. But this, relatively, was a small thing: for religious disbarment meant the loss of serenity in this world, and, above all, of hope for the next and for the day of resurrection. Joachim, angry and humiliated, feeling that he had been unjustly singled out for banishment from the Holy Places, reacted vigorously and sought to defend himself by searching in the Scrolls to discover whether the 'Histories of the Twelve Tribes of Israel' would not furnish contrary precedents, and other examples of childlessness which had been allowed to pass without such grievous punishment. But he found that 'All the righteous had raised up offspring' and concluded that he was 'the only one [of the righteous] who has not raised up offspring in Israel'. He remembered that when the great patriarch Abraham was old and nearing the end of his life, God had given him a son, Isaac; but Joachim was not Abraham, and after twenty years of a childless marriage, he could hardly hope for so great a boon.

In the heat of the moment he blamed his wife for all his troubles. And without any warning to her he went off to the hill country, to the solitary places where his shepherds and herdsmen were with his cattle, and there he pitched his tent and fasted, grieving. Like Moses on the mountain and Jesus in the wilderness, he fasted for forty days and forty nights, praying to God for understanding and mercy and relief in *22* his distress and offering up burnt sacrifice. Miraculously, his prayers
8 *18* were answered. One day, as he slept, an angel came to awaken him and to tell him that the Almighty had seen fit to pity him and to grant him the prospect of fatherhood. He should quit his hillside forthwith, return to his wife, and all would be well.

Meanwhile Anne had remained at home, where the news of her husband's disgrace and the manner of his departure from Jerusalem was quickly reported to her. Throughout their marriage her barrenness had been her affliction, and sometimes her shame; and now it seemed that it had brought disaster to her husband, and to their whole house. And Joachim had departed—where, she did not know—without a word or a message to her. Suddenly, almost from one hour to the next, she found herself an outcast from the church and abandoned by her husband. Her fall was great. Even her servants and slaves, reacting *14* quickly to her new situation, openly mocked her. She dressed only in mourning garments. But eventually the day of the Passover arrived when it was not proper for a woman, even in the privacy of her own house, to appear in mourning; and dressing herself, as was her custom

14 Anne in her garden, with a pouting servant and the nesting sparrows. The angel announces the birth to come. On the right can be seen the annunciation to Joachim. Mosaic in a church at Daphne, Greece, eleventh century.

on great feast days, in her wedding robe, she went out in the afternoon into the cool of the garden and sat down beside a stream under the shade of a laurel tree.

14   It was springtime, and looking up into the branches above her she saw a sparrow's nest, and the parent birds flying to and fro feeding their young. Even they, she thought, can have offspring, and she gave way to her despair:

> Woe to me, who begot me,
> What womb brought me forth?
> For I was born as a curse before them all and before the
>   children of Israel,
> And I was reproached and they mocked me and they thrust
>   me out of the Temple of the Lord.
>
> Woe to me, to what am I likened?
> I am not likened to the birds of the heaven;
> For even the birds of the heaven are fruitful before thee,
>   O Lord.

I am not likened to the dumb animals,
For even the dumb animals are fruitful before thee, O Lord . . .
I am not likened to these waters,
For even these waters gush forth merrily, and their fish
    praise thee, O Lord.

Woe to me, to what am I likened?
I am not likened to this earth;
For even this earth brings forth its fruit in season, and praises
    thee, O Lord.

Her lament was a despairing invocation, and it brought a miraculous
14 answer: 'Behold, the angel of the Lord came to her, and said, "Anne,
Anne, the Lord has heard your prayer. You shall conceive and bear,
and your offspring shall be spoken of in the whole world"'. Anne, in
a sudden surge of joy, answered, 'As the Lord my God lives, if I bear a
child, whether it be male or female, I will bring it as a gift to the Lord
my God, and it shall serve Him all the days of its life.'
92   Husband and wife had been visited simultaneously by the celestial
messengers and Joachim, pausing only to make a burnt offering to God,
set off immediately for Jerusalem, driving before him—for he knew
that soon he would no longer be barred from the Temple—the choicest
beasts from his flocks, so that when the time came he might offer them
to the altar of sacrifice in a holocaust of gratitude. He sent two messengers before him to warn his wife of his return, and she, receiving
them with joy and loading them with gifts, went out to meet her
husband before the great gate of the city, for they had told her that
their master and his men had followed not many miles behind them.
Her wait was long. But 'when she was growing faint with long expectation, she raised her eyes and saw Joachim afar off coming with his
23 flocks: and she met him, and hung upon his neck, giving thanks to
God, and saying "I was a widow, and Lo, I am not one now"'.
      Of the immediate sequel to this happy meeting we know no more
than that 'Joachim rested the first day in his house', that Anne conceived
and Joachim was readmitted to the Temple; and that eventually a girl
19 child was born to them whom they called Mary. The coming of this
child had been announced to each of the parents by divine messengers,
and we know that this was the child who was to be the Virgin Mother
of Jesus, the Mother of God. But as yet there is no suggestion that
any special circumstances had attended her begetting; which brings
us to a point in the story which is delicate in the extreme, for in later
centuries the conception of Mary was required to have a far more
subtle character: to be, in fact, the 'Immaculate' conception. At

this stage, we are far from this ideal. The whole of the preceding narrative has been taken from the Protevangelium of James, the oldest of the 'Infancy' texts which, as one would expect, places the least emphasis on the special qualities and special character of Mary, who for some centuries in the East and for a millennium in the West was a comparatively secondary personage, of infinitely less importance than her son.

Nevertheless James's story of the birth of Mary was soon to prove insufficient. In the East, Marialism as a mystic and ecstatic force flowered early, perhaps as early as the sixth century. One of its simpler manifestations is the Gospel of Pseudo-Matthew, a later apocryphal work which was known to Jerome in *c.* 400, but in the form in which we know it dates probably from the eighth century. This work drew heavily on the Protevangelium and other early sources, but arranged and expanded their material to give exceptional prominence and exceptional sanctity to the person of Mary the Perpetual Virgin; though even here the manner of her begetting as the natural child of her parents remains essentially unchanged. In the Eastern Church Mary may already have been held to have been altogether sinless in her life, for the concept of her as the new Eve and of Jesus as the recreated Adam is a very ancient one which goes back to the early Fathers of the Church; but it is clear that even as late as the tenth century, Byzantine theological subtlety had not yet so much as adumbrated the doctrine of the Immaculate Conception.

Precisely when and where the concept was evolved we do not know, but less than two centuries later—though it was still disputed by, for example, the Schoolmen—it was current as an exact formula throughout Christendom, and its ingenious mechanics had been resolved. There existed, fortunately, a minor apocryphal work, the Gospel of the Nativity of Mary, which in the form in which we know it is probably still later than Pseudo-Matthew, and which is essentially a pietistic treatise in praise of Mary herself. Even here, however, the 'conception' is a normal one and the basic story follows that of the earlier Infancy gospels. The annunciatory angel even says to Joachim, 'Anne thy wife shall bear thee a daughter and you shall call her name Mary, and she shall be consecrated to the Lord from her infancy.' But in this text, and as far as we know for the first time, the meeting of Joachim and Anne was defined as taking place at a 'Golden Gate', which was supposed by some to have been a gate of special sanctity in the walls of Jerusalem, and by others to have been the gate of the Temple itself. They had surely been reunited, then, in a holy place, on holy ground sanctified by God. And once this point was accepted it was no great leap forward to formulate, and eventually to establish, the theory

that on this spot they had exchanged a chaste, and holy, and pro-
23 creative kiss which had breathed into the mother's womb the concept
and the substance of Mary her daughter; a kiss which precluded the
need for any physical act of generation. We shall consider the implications of this more fully in Chapter 12, but we can be sure that to enun-
ciate a theory was to believe its truth. This could not but have been the
work of Heaven. The link with the old Adam had been broken, and
Mary freed from the taint of original sin.

With the growth of Marial fervour in the later Middle Ages, this
'Kiss at the Golden Gate' became a popular subject in the art of both
the East and the West. In the Byzantine and the later Russian traditions,
which usually set the scene at the gate of the Temple, and in the art of
the West, which opted for a gate in the walls of Jerusalem, it is generally
shown as no more than a chaste embrace, without any suggestion of a
meeting of lips. Where an actual kiss is intended—and this occurs
only in the West, and almost never in artifacts other than at the Golden
Gate—an angel hovers above the couple, bringing their faces together
with its hands, emphasising by its heaven-sent gesture the sacred and
creative nature of this special marital salute.

Throughout the later mediaeval centuries the belief held firm that
this famous kiss lay at the first begetting of Mary and had been the
breath of life from which she grew. But at the Reformation the Calvinists
and the Reformed Churches in general would have little truck with
such matters; and the Council of Trent, for its part, swept them all
away, holding them an inadequate basis for the initial sanctity of the
Queen of Heaven. The Roman church evolved an Immaculate Conception
of another form and by the year 1854, when at last the concept became
dogma, it was held to proceed solely from the apprehension that 'from
the very first moment of her conception the Blessed Virgin Mary was,
by the singular grace and privilege of Almighty God, and in view of
the merits of Jesus Christ, Saviour of mankind, kept free from all stain
of original sin'. This may be more sublime than the idea of old Joachim
and Anne at the Golden Gate. But some might hold, with the mediaeval
Schoolmen, that it begs the question; and more might regret that the
ancient and picturesque tale was finally supplanted by a theological
fiat.

2 The childhood and marriage of Mary

19 And her months were fulfilled as the angel had said: in the ninth month Anne brought forth. And she said to the midwife: 'What have I brought forth?' And she said, 'A female.' And Anne said: 'My soul is magnified this day.' And she lay down. And when the days were fulfilled, Anne purified herself from her childbed and gave suck to the child, and called her Mary.

11 Anne's barrenness of twenty years was over, and the shame which she had brought to her husband and her family was ended. She had not borne a son, that most desired of blessings, but she had had a child whose coming had been foretold by angels and who surely awaited an exceptional destiny which would add lustre to the great house of Joachim. Anne might well exult:

I will sing praises to the Lord my God,
For he has visited me and taken away from me the
    reproach of my enemies.
And the Lord gave me the fruit of righteousness,
    unique and manifold before him.
Who will proclaim to the sons of Reuben that Anne
    gives suck?
Hearken, hearken, you twelve tribes of Israel!
    Anne gives suck!

Day by day, we are told, the child grew stronger. When she was only six months old Anne, in a mother's very human gesture, 'stood her on the ground to try if she could stand. And she took twice seven

opposite
15 When the pregnancy of Mary has become common knowledge, her sinlessness is put to the test of the 'Trial by Water'. From a series of Italian drawings illustrating the life of the Virgin and Christ, *c.* 1400.

overleaf
16 Joachim and Anne giving alms to beggars at their gate. Stained glass window at Chalons-sur-Marne, France, 1527.

Qualiter sctus Joachim pater beate marie cū sua oblatōne fuit repulsus a tēplo a sūmo pontifice Judeorum

steps and returned to her'. Anne was already persuaded, as all mothers are, of the exceptional character of her baby; and her own strong religious feelings, together with the signs of divine favour which had preceded the birth of her child, led her to surround this infant Mary, from her earliest days, with an aura of sanctity: 'She took her up, saying, as the Lord my God lives, you shall no more walk on the ground until I take you to the Temple of the Lord. And she made a sanctuary of her bedchamber and did not permit anything common or unclean to pass through it'. Mary was already a being set apart. Her feet, lest they be defiled by earthly contact, were not to be allowed to touch the ground until they walked on the holy ground of the Temple; her nursery was already a sanctuary. Here, in the earliest of the apocryphal books, we find the history, and the particularly sacred character of Mary expanding, taking shape, and emerging from its narrow biblical envelope. The Protevangelium, like the books of the New Testament, is a Levantine document; and it is already preparing the way for the rise of Marialism in the Byzantine east.

In these days of her infancy, the 'undefiled daughters of the Hebrews'—whom we shall meet again—cared for her amusement; and on the child's first birthday her father Joachim gave a feast on a scale which only he, perhaps, could have contrived. For this first anniversary he invited not only the chief priests, and the priests, and the scribes, and the elders, but 'the whole people of Israel'. The chief priests, of course, gave the babe their blessing, and Anne her mother, as befitted a woman and the mistress of the house, waited on their table. And when the feast was over they 'went down rejoicing and glorifying the God of Israel'. Mary had been well launched into the world, and brought early to the notice of those who were to be her mentors.

The months passed, the child grew, and by the time that her second birthday had come round her parents, mindful of Anne's vows, considered sending her to the Temple for her future upbringing. Joachim felt that the time for this had already come, but Anne, with a mother's solicitude for so small a child, urged that she should remain at home for another year. And she won her point. The move was made

overleaf
17 Joachim's offering is refused—the High Priest Reuben drives him from the Temple. Fresco in the church of S. Croce, Florence, by Giovanni da Milano, mid-fourteenth century.

opposite
18 Joachim is awakened from his dreams by the angel. Fresco in the Capello Scrovegni, Padua, by Giotto, *c.* 1305.

on the third birthday. Thorough preparations had been made for her reception at the Sanctuary, and the parents and their predestined child set out from the house to walk in procession to the Temple, followed not only by their kinsmen and their household retainers but, in an ancient Greek tradition, by seven virgins bearing lamps: or, as we might think of them, by seven bridesmaids following this bride to her first, her true marriage to the House of God. And so they approached the Temple of Jerusalem, that holiest of places which had been chosen for her education and for her upbringing in the fear of the Lord.

20 24

19 The birth of Mary: Joachim is kneeling in the foreground, looking at the child. Attributed to Hans Baldund Grien, *c.* 1500.

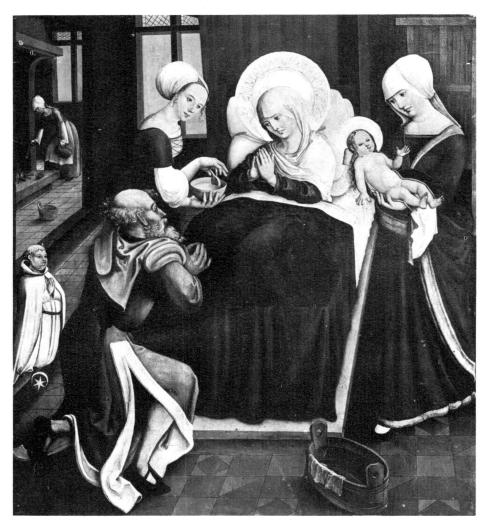

This was a curious arrangement; and we must remember that we are drawing our information from documents of which the earliest date from the second century, by which time most of the members of the fledgling Christian church were tending to forget the Jewish origin of their faith which Paul, in its earliest days, had striven so hard to preserve. That the writers of a later day should have wished to associate Mary with the great Temple was understandable. That sacred fortress, that marvel of the Roman world, had disappeared in the first Christian century, never to rise again from its ashes. But its memory was holy, enshrined in the Old Testament books and in sacred sentiment, and an emotional but confused recollection of it was always present in their minds and figured constantly in their writings; just as it was to haunt the western world throughout the history of Christianity. It was thought of as unparalleled in the ancient world, and it lay at the heart of the religion of Jesus. It was repeatedly invoked in the prayers of Christians; the Muslims held that from its site Muhammed had ascended to Heaven; and the holy places which lay within its ruined walls were the ostensible reason for the Crusades. Its image, perhaps a little confused, has persisted in the substratum of western thought and we find it even today in the hymns of the northern churches which invoke so often this citadel of Zion which became the Temple of Jehovah, the great defensive bastion, the fort and holy place of ancient Jewry which David first captured from the Jebusites and made into his city, 'David's city', set in the western flank of the walls of Jerusalem.

But the nature of the ceremonies, the constitution and the organisation of this great 'city'—in the full ancient sense of that term—had been soon forgotten. In fact, the Temple never had a school for Mary to go to. It would never have housed young girls within its massive walls. The Christians, taught by their apocryphal books, thought otherwise, and the tradition was strong and lasting, so that in mediaeval and even Renaissance artifacts we can sometimes see the actual pupils, carefully separated into boy's school and girl's school, watching with interest and excitement the arrival of their illustrious recruit. This was an attractive, a genial invention. It was part of a tradition which served practical, as well as devotional ends, and created a framework for the detailed knowledge, which was once so much cherished, of the childhood and the upbringing of the one who was to be the mother of Jesus. And this Temple, after all, was soon to see her marriage.

We are told that Mary, once the procession had reached its precincts and she saw her new, her holier life before her, left her parents without a backward glance. She ran up the steps of the Grand Stairway of the Temple and into the welcoming arms of the High Priest waiting above.

20 Three scenes from the life of Mary: her coronation, flanked by the dedication to the Temple (left) and the birth of Jesus (right). By Antonio Vivarini, active 1440–76.

It was later believed that there were fifteen of these steps, and that they had symbolised the fifteen 'Psalms of Degrees'—Psalms CXX to CXXXIV—which the Jewish people in their joy had chanted when, on their return from the long exile of Babylon, they had come again within sight of the walls of Jerusalem. This number was almost always respected by the many painters of the West—but not of the East—who depicted this scene, and it is interesting to count the steps that they show, and to remember these Psalms. In the great galleries of the world these pictures are almost always labelled not as the 'Dedication of Mary', but, oddly, as her 'Presentation to the Temple', a ceremony which was not performed for girl children, and which, if an exception had been made in this special case, would have taken place long before.

Once she was within the Temple, the High Priest 'placed her on the third step of the altar, and the Lord God put grace upon the child, and she danced for joy with her feet, and the whole house of Israel loved her.' A charming first glimpse of Mary the predestined child; who now, in the House of God, was to be surrounded by daily wonders. She was 'nurtured like a dove and fed by angels'; and in the art of the Eastern church we can often see her, a small and rather lonely figure set in an elevated ambo, to whom an angel from on high is fluttering down, bringing her little flat breads, usually in the form of chapattis, which seem to have been her only food.

24

It is to this period of her life that the church, and particularly the Eastern church, attributes a story of which an element was to become one of her main characteristics and one of her main recognition symbols in the Middle Ages. The curtains of the Sanctuary, of the Holy of Holies, which alone of all the hangings of the Temple were of the 'True Purple' colour, were renewed every year, and the spinning and the weaving of the cloth were granted to one of the girls of the Temple school who was chosen by lot to perform this task. In her year, the lot 25 fell upon Mary, so that it was she to whom this particularly sacred labour was entrusted. She was still the youngest pupil, and her fellow students, who all would spin in other colours and have other tasks to perform, were jealous of her privilege and became spiteful towards her; but Mary won them over 'by the modesty of her attitude and the sweetness of her nature'; so that they too, it was said, came to love her. This story, in the attenuated form of Mary the Mother of God who yet span her wool as every housewife did, soon spread to the West, and was everywhere of particular comfort to toiling womankind. In a thousand artifacts, ranging in time from the early works of Byzantium to the great bronze doors of Hildesheim or Novgorod, and on to the Renaissance, in Italy, we can see her with her symbolic spindle and sometimes with her loom. Holy Mary, Mary the woman, is spinning; 21 68 spinning, perhaps, the True Purple of the Holy of Holies; but spinning all the same.

The years of her life in the Temple passed quickly and at length, at the age of twelve — or, as some said, of fourteen — she became a young woman, and nubile. The tone of the story changes abruptly. From having been the *persona maxissima grata* of the Temple, sanctified and sanctifying, she became an adolescent inhabitant whom it was impossible to keep longer within the sacred walls. 'What shall we do with her', said the priests, 'that she may not pollute the Temple of the Lord?' It was urgent that she should leave the precincts and therefore, it seems, urgent that she should be married. No one suggested that she should return to the parents whom she had left so blithely, nor do her parents appear to have visited her at any time during her years at the Temple school; and indeed, as far as the early apocryphal stories are concerned, Joachim and Anne disappear from our sight at the foot of the Fifteen Steps. Mary, at this critical juncture in her life, appears to be curiously alone in a terrestrial and masculine world. In the event, the Chief Priest himself assumed a parental role, and putting on his 'vestment with the twelve bells', entered the Sanctuary and prayed for guidance in the choice of a husband for the young girl. An angel appeared, and instructed him to 'go out and assemble the widowers of the people, who each shall bring a rod, and to whomever the Lord shall give a miraculous sign, his wife shall she be'.

The fiat went out, the trumpets sounded, and the ram's horns were blown from the walls of the Temple. At the signal, the single men, as they were required to do, came running, their staves in their hands; and Joseph the Carpenter, appearing for the first time on the scene of the world, 'threw down his axe and went to meet them. And when they were gathered together, they took their rods and went to the High Priest.' According to the Protevangelium, the High Priest gathered up their 'rods', their personal staves, and went into the Temple with them and prayed; and came out again with the rods in his arms and distributed them to the waiting men, giving each staff to its owner. Joseph received his the last: 'And behold, a dove came out

21 The tradition of 'Mary spinning' was carried on until at least the date of this late-seventeenth-century engraving by Jacques Bellange.

of the rod and flew on to Joseph's head. And the priest said to Joseph, "Joseph, to you has fallen the good fortune to receive the virgin of the Lord: take her under your care"'. Pseudo-Matthew, however, which was the source from which the late Middle Ages took most of their information on these matters, elaborates and dramatises the story. When the men brought their staves to the High Priest he, acting under heavenly guidance, placed them for the night on a table behind the high altar in the Holy of Holies. They were to be redistributed in the courtyard of the Temple early the next day, and the familiar angel had announced that the staff of the chosen bridegroom would bud, and the sign of a dove would appear. But in the morning nothing happened, there was no dove, and the High Priest returned to the altar for further guidance. The angel duly manifested itself again and said, 'There is a very short rod which yesterday you placed with the others, but which you took this morning to be of no account, leaving it where it lay. When you have taken it out and given it to whom it belongs, then shall the sign appear'. The rod, of course, was Joseph's, and he, in this late work, was said to have been an old man who, though he had obeyed the signal for assembly, had been too modest to claim his staff again, too modest to stand in contention for the hand of this young virgin. 'He stood humble and the last. The Chief Priest with a loud voice cried to him, saying, "Come, Joseph, and receive your rod, for you are waited for". And Joseph came fearing, for the High Priest had called him with so very loud a voice. But he stretched out his hand to receive the rod, and immediately a dove went forth from its top, whiter than snow and most beautiful, and fluttering a long time among the pinnacles of the Temple, it flew at last towards the heavens'.

Against all probability, he was the man. An astounded and reticent Joseph pleads his seniority and his inappropriateness as a husband for so young a bride. But he cannot disobey God's sign, God's will: and he is instructed to take her back to his house until the time when, as he himself says with a thought of future relief, he could know by a sign from Heaven which of his sons should take her for his bride. But this would not have been possible within the law, and in the special circumstances of the case, the priest decreed that five virgins should be given to Mary as her companions 'until the day appointed comes when you shall take her, for she cannot be joined to another in matrimony.' The five virgins — Rebecca, Zipporah, Suzanna, Abigail and Cael, the 'undefiled daughters of the Hebrews' — were chosen, and they all returned together to Joseph's home, where in Pseudo-Matthew they spun the coloured wools, with Mary, of course, working on the True Purple. In this way Mary spent her time in the company of women with no man near her, for Joseph was an itinerant worker and immediately he had settled the little party in his house he left them 'to make tabernacles in the Maritime Provinces, for he was a carpenter'.

The first days of Joseph and Mary are not always presented in this way. Early versions of the tale which are still available to us tell much the same story as Pseudo-Matthew, but in the late mediaeval centuries, the centuries of the most fervent Marialism, it was held that once the dove had appeared which designated Joseph as the husband-elect, a *31* real, a 'church' marriage took place immediately. Many artifacts show the scene: the High Priest officiates, and sometimes the wedding is sanctified by the simple joining of hands before him. Sometimes, from another tradition — or perhaps because, in some countries a true churching could not be imagined in any other way — Joseph slips a ring on Mary's finger; and often the tip of his staff flowers quite extravagantly, and the miraculous dove flies off from among the blooms and the foliage. Often, the pictures show us the unlucky suitors, *27 32* angered by missing so great a prize, breaking their unfecund rods across their knees and threatening him with their fists, or actually buffeting him in the presence of the priest and during the ceremony of the marriage. But now there was nothing that they could do to change the course of destiny; and after the wedding Joseph returned to his house with his young spouse and the stage was set for the unfolding of events which for almost two millennia have reverberated about the world.

Here, we should digress for a moment. There is little doubt but that knowledge of this event, this churching, was solid and widespread in the Middle Ages and that this knowledge was based on early texts no longer available to us. If this had not have been the case the many pictures showing this marriage would not have been ordered by the men who bespoke them. As we have seen in the Introduction, mediaeval religious painting was didactic. Its subjects were reminders of familiar and entirely accepted events, and served to recall, in their secondary and deeper meaning, religious tenets and subjects for meditation. It was not the business of a religious institution or of a rich patron to

opposite
22 Joachim's burnt offering to God, whose hand is in the sky — the angel announces that Anne will bear a child. Fresco in the Capello Scrovegni, Padua, by Giotto, *c.* 1305.

overleaf
23 The re-uniting of Joachim and Anne: their Kiss at the Golden Gate. 'When she was growing faint with very long expectation she raised her eyes and saw Joachim afar off coming with his flocks; and she met him, and hung upon his neck, saying, I was a widow: and Lo! I am not one now'. By the 'Master of the Life of Mary', *c.* 1480.

order, under any circumstances, the depiction of a religious scene which did not accord with accepted tradition and it was certainly not the business of the artisan to invent or even to embroider on a basic theme. And in East and West alike, significant variation from the traditional theme and presentation was heresy.

These conventions are valuable to us. The primary aim of this book is to set out the biblical and apocryphal account of the ancestors and early life of Jesus and to examine mediaeval artifacts associated with this complex story. The distinction in our own minds between the biblical and the apocryphal is sharp, and at first sight appears to be that between holy writ and secular invention. But mediaeval man did not know the Bible. He knew stories but not their sources. Even the ablest men of the time had little historical discrimination, little sense of the passage of times past, and none of the selective gathering of information. Men lived in a world of speech. Few, very few, can have had the faintest apprehension that this story which they knew so well, of Jesus and his mother was strung together from many sources and from many lands, that some of it descended from tales of more ancient Gods and a little of it, perhaps, from fertile imaginations. For them all of it was hallowed alike by time and long belief. All alike was sacred and indisputable. Biblical and apocryphal stood together, on the same plane, and Mary had woven the True Purple just as surely as her son had raised Lazurus from the dead. The illustrations of craftsmen were created for no other purpose than to remind men of the way in which it was believed that things had happened.

When we see, then, a picture of the actual 'church' marriage of Joseph and Mary we know that in the area and time of the picture's origin it was quite naturally accepted that the event had been a real one and that the picture demonstrates, and celebrates, the story of

3   *overleaf above*
24 A Byzantine 'Dedication': Mary's parents and the Seven Virgins accompany her to the Temple, where she is received by the High Priest; she is also shown seated in the ambo and fed by an angel. Mosaic in the Kariye Camii, Istanbul, fourteenth century.

overleaf below
25 The distribution of the coloured wools to the girls of the Temple School: Mary receives the 'True Purple', though in the picture the colour has faded with time. Mosaic in the Kariye Camii, Istanbul, fourteenth century.

opposite
26 A western 'Dedication'. Mary walks up the fifteen steps, looking towards her future companion. Above are other pupils: boys to the right, girls to the left. The fresco, in the church of S. Croce, Florence, is by Giovanni da Milano, *c.* 1470.

27 The marriage of Joseph and Mary, by Domenico Ghirlandaio, 1449–94.

how it had come about. This fact can lead to a fortunate extension of our knowledge. As we have already seen, a considerable proportion of mediaeval 'biblical' art shows scenes, or details of scenes, which have no place in the Bible. Most of these can be traced quite easily to the apocryphal texts. Some we cannot yet decipher. But sometimes a picture or group of pictures will show us a scene which can be clearly identified — by, for example, the place which it holds in a group of sequential scenes — but for which we have no written source; and so adds to our apocryphal knowledge. In this book, and in a number of cases, scenes or details of scenes have been written into the text because artifacts, and artifacts alone, show us that once men believed that these things had happened, and had happened thus. This may seem erratic, or unduly venturesome, but we believe it to be perfectly legitimate. We have to remember that we are dealing, not with the tabulated and scientific world of today, but with mediaeval concepts and mediaeval beliefs which sprung from thought processes marvellously different from our own; and which had their own rules which changed at no more than a pace dictated by the extreme conservatism of the time. A picture was a picture. What it showed, had happened.

3 The home of Joseph

After the wedding, with its dove, its flowering rods, and its singular portents of events to come, Joseph returned home with his young bride, and the apocryphal authors, who are telling tales of pious wonder generally untroubled by logical considerations, find themselves confronted by a situation which was hard even for them to handle. Mary is now, by definition, nubile. She has had to leave the Temple precincts lest they should be menstrually defiled; she is said in the various apocryphals to be between twelve and fifteen years old, which were entirely acceptable ages for marriage in biblical society; and within a year she will bear a child. Moreover, she has been wedded to a man who is pious and kind, and whom some held to be elderly; she has returned to his house as his bride; and, according to any reasonable reading of canonical Matthew and Mark, she is later to bear him sons and daughters. But Mary has already been marked out by repeated portents as a special personage with a special destiny, and for the moment she must not only be, but must remain and be seen to remain a virgin. Ideally, she should be freed even from the taint of masculine presence about her person.

We have seen Pseudo-Matthew's solution to the problem in the provision of the five 'undefiled daughters of the Hebrews' who kept her company and guarded her from any suggestion of a husband's attentions. The idea of this feminine bulwark was generally remembered in the Orthodox lands, but in the West it seems to have carried little weight. The prevailing view was that Joseph merely installed Mary in his home, and leaving her alone in her new quarters, departed forthwith to go about his business as an itinerant carpenter and to make the rounds which kept him from home for many months at a time. To close the circle of virginity round her more securely, and to answer for the short time which she must necessarily have spent with her husband after the wedding, Mary was said to have been given to him 'in trust' and so to be unviolable under the law until she should be older. No such semi-marital status existed in fact under the Judaic law, and this 'in trust' condition was probably an invention of

28 After the wedding, Joseph returns to his home with Mary. Mosaic in the Kariye
Camii, Istanbul, fourteenth century.

the Apologists of the early Christian centuries. But it is an important point, for it was held to have imposed legal and moral restraints upon Joseph which will have considerable significance later in our tale.

Luke, and Luke alone among the Evangelists, in his 'Annunciation' passage takes up a version of the story: Mary the virgin was in Joseph's house in distant Galilee, and there the angel Gabriel appeared to her, apostrophising her as one highly favoured, and blessed among women. He told her:

. . . thou hast found favour with God.
And, behold, thou shalt conceive in thy womb, and bring forth a son, and shalt call his name JESUS.
He shall be great, and shall be called the Son of the Highest: and the Lord God shall give him the throne of his father David: and he shall reign over the house of Jacob for ever; and of his kingdom there shall be no end.

Mary, the flockmaster's daughter, the carpenter's wife, could by no means comprehend so great an honour, or the means by which it could be brought about; but Gabriel assured her that:

The Holy Ghost shall come upon thee, and the power of the Highest shall overshadow thee; therefore also that holy thing which shall be born of thee shall be called the Son of God.

This, then, was what was to happen. It was a command, and for her that was enough. It was the ways of men. She bowed before them, and awaited her destiny: *'Behold the handmaid of the Lord; be it unto me according to the word.'* In the dignity of this response, this serene acceptance of her future, we can begin to apprehend, in this little startled Jewish child, the first adumbration of the great Queen of Heaven.

The matter, the mystery, might well have been allowed to remain there, to be accepted as something beyond the comprehension of men; but mediaeval theologians, mediaeval divines, could leave nothing well alone. Jesus was to be born a man-God, with a human as well as a divine nature, so a masculine element was considered altogether necessary for his creation. With biblical authority, it was easy to contend that this was furnished by the Holy Spirit. But it was deemed essential to know exactly how this came about. It was held by many divines that the Holy Ghost, at the time of the Annunciation, penetrated Mary's body in an unusual way and there physically implanted the male element of Jesus' conception. There was much speculation as to

30 A classical 'Annunciation'. Detail from the Ghent Altarpiece, St Bavon, Ghent, by Jan van Eyck, 1432.

the path which had been followed in this fecundation, the gestatory period which divided the Annunciation from the birth, and the precise moment during Mary's pregnancy at which God's essence became sufficiently formed to be deemed a man, and a God. The path, it was finally agreed, was through the right ear, and the gestatory period a normal nine months. The last question was never settled to the general satisfaction, and periods of three, and six, months from the Annunciation, and even the actual moment of birth, were advanced and

opposite

29 The Annunciation to Mary, by the 'Master of the Virgo inter Virgines', *c.* 1480.

debated upon by these mediaeval churchmen, with their compulsive need to systematise their theological speculations and to give a recognisable, almost a scientific form even to the most arcane concepts.

For the vulgar, actual physical representations were necessary. A number of paintings still exist, in which the actual child, already perfectly formed in the mind of God, is shown descending the direct path between the physical presence of the Almighty, and the Virgin's ear; while others show Mary as a normally pregnant woman whose nine-month time has come. This habit of concretisation, of visualisation of everything from the sacred mysteries to the minutiae of theology, reached what was perhaps its highest point in the ingenious 'Vierges Ouvrantes', which were made from the thirteenth century until at least the sixteenth: statues of the pregnant Mary, with little doors let into the lower part of her back which one can open to discover, and abstract, a tiny, perfectly formed child. An unborn Jesus lies in one's hand, taken from his mother's womb; and one can imagine priests of other days showing this little object to the faithful as a tangible proof of the One who was born as they were, but who ever will Be.

The apocryphal writers were not concerned with such curious manifestations of devotion, and they placed the Annunciation to Mary, and her subsequent pregnancy, on another plane. We find Mary as a young bride, left alone in a house which must have been quite unfamiliar to her, and presumably fending for herself in all things. One morning, she had gone out with her bucket to draw water from the well in the inner courtyard when suddenly an angel—or, in some accounts, simply a 'young man'—appeared before her. He began to tell her that he was a messenger from God, but the poor girl, terrified— as well she might have been—by this apparition, ran back to hide herself in the house. The angel followed her, and delivered an 'Annunciation' similar to the one with which we are so familiar from the words of Luke, and to which she eventually replied in kind. But in these apocryphal accounts Mary, who after all was hardly more than a little girl, seems to have been unable to recognise the importance and the celestial validity of the remarkable message, and the texts have it that after the departure of the angel she reacted as, quite simply, a

opposite
31 Mary's many suitors, and the vigil of the rods. Only Joseph's flowers and he is married to Mary. By L. von Brixen, *c.* 1463.

overleaf
32 The trumpets blow for the marriage of Joseph and Mary, while the disappointed suitors break the rods and buffet Joseph. Fresco by Fra Angelico in S. Marco, Florence, *c.* 1436.

frightened child. She did not appear to comprehend the true import of anything which the heavenly messenger had said, or to understand in any way what had happened to her; and when, a little time later, she found herself pregnant, she was horrified. Her husband was, and had been, away. She may have grasped something of the unique nature of her case, but she was alone, and the strange messenger had spoken to her alone. She knew that in the eyes of the world, or at least in the eyes of her husband, her pregnancy could mean only one thing: adultery. And the punishment for adultery was death.

In her great trouble Mary thought of Elizabeth the wife of Zacharias. Joseph, it was said, was her cousin, and she knew that Elizabeth, also, though a much older woman than herself, was pregnant for the first time. It seems that she lived in or somewhere quiet close to Bethlehem, and Mary, greatly daring, slipped out one night to visit her and implore her help. She was welcomed with joy, the women talked together for a long time, and in what is perhaps a late addition to one of the apocryphal accounts, Elizabeth perceived and gloried in the special nature of her cousin's pregnancy; and Mary responds to her with a hymn comparable with the Magnificat. But at the end of this 'Visitation' Elizabeth, realising perhaps the hopelessness of the cause of a young girl who has to convince the world of men that she is with child of the Holy Spirit, has no better advice to give her than that she should go back home, try to conceal her condition, and hope for the best.

So she returned to her house; but when Joseph came back from his journey Mary's condition was already such that he recognised it at once for what it was, and called down terrible maledictions on her head, and on his own. He knew that a pregnant wife could not be hid for long, and that the first suspicions of his neighbours, and of the rulers of the church, would be that before he had left on his travels he had violated his 'trust', and his young bride. He felt already the injustice of his case, for he knew his own innocence, and he could make nothing of the extraordinary story of angelic visitations which Mary tried to tell him. There was, though, at least something which could be done. As in Matthew's account of the matter, Joseph, *being a just man, and not willing to make her a public example, was minded to put her away privily:* or, that she be not stoned for adultery, to send her away to bear her child in some place where she was not known. But, in the apocryphals as in the canon, he was deterred from doing so

33 The Visitation of Mary to Elizabeth, who touches the pregnant Mary tenderly with her hand. Stained-glass window at Chalons-sur-Marne, France, sixteenth century.

34 The first Annunciation, at the well in the courtyard of Joseph's house. Detail from the Werden casket.

by an angelic messenger who came to him in a dream and told him that Mary was bearing the child of the Holy Spirit. This revelation he *37* accepted without question, and in the morning he saw Mary with other eyes; but it had been made to him alone, in a dream; and his personal situation, the guilt he must bear before the world, remained unchanged.

Joseph's anger and resentment when he returns from his journey to find his young wife pregnant, and his inability to make head or tail of her story of the divine messenger and the Holy Ghost, was a popular subject in the Middle Ages and the Miracle Plays extracted a good deal of knockabout humour from the situation. A late, a fifteenth-century version of the Nativity play from the Chester Miracle Cycle treats the scene in this way:

(Joseph dixit) . . . Three monethes shee hath bine from me
Now hasse she gotten her, as I see
A great belly like to thee
Syth she went away.

And myne it is not, bee thou bould
For I am both ould and could.
These thirty winters, though I would
I might not playe noe playe.

God, never lett ould man
Take to wife a yonge woman
Nay seet his harte her upon
Lest he beguyled bee . . .

In the East, Joseph's suspicion and anger was held to have lasted until after the coming of Jesus, and Byzantine pictures sometimes show the Devil talking to him at the scene of the birth and stirring up his sense of wrong.

But to return to our story. Whatever Joseph might have planned to do to conceal the plight of Mary it was too late, for the unhappy pair were overtaken by events. We know that Joseph feared that, for all his reputation for piety and discretion, others would mock the story of heavenly messengers; and when at the third hour of the day a church elder came to the house to welcome him back after his journey he kept his wife as far as possible in the shadows, made no mention of his dream, and hoped that nothing would be noticed. But the visitor, who well knew the special circumstances of the marriage, had seen enough to suspect Mary's condition, and though he made no comment as he left the house, he went straight to the High Priest and told him what he thought he had seen. The Priest was at first incredulous, for he knew Joseph to be a pillar of the church and a firm upholder of the law. But the accusation had been made and the matter could not be allowed to lie. Mary must be seen in the full light of day; and a detachment of men was ordered to Joseph's house with instructions to bring the pair to the judgment chamber of the Temple.

There Mary's pregnant state was to be seen only too clearly. Joseph protested his innocence but was reduced to silence by the evidence; and from fear of ridicule, perhaps, he still made no attempt to defend his own reputation, and his bride's, by any mention of the heavenly messengers which had appeared to each of them. Mary's own insistence before her judges that she had known no man seemed to be not loyalty to her husband, but a manifest and impious lie which added to the weight of her sin. However, Joseph had many friends at court, and his reputation for piety was such that, rather than condemn the pair out of hand, the High Priest allowed them to undergo the 'Trial by the Water of the Conviction of the Lord', an invocation of Divine judgment which might be compared with the trials by fire and water of the high Middle Ages. In the Temple ordinance, the accused was given a magical liquid to drink, and then compelled—as far as we can understand it—to take some form of physical exercise, which in the Coventry Corpus Christi play took the form of running

35 Joseph and the Trial by Water. From a series of Italian drawings illustrating the Life of the Virgin and Christ, *c.* 1400.

36 Reflective, majestic and calm, Mary awaits the birth of her child. By Piero della Francesca, fifteenth century.

seven times round the altar. If either party was guilty of the specific crime invoked, a sign of condemnation would appear, and be clear to all: and the judgement of the 'water' was sovereign.

15 35 42 Joseph and Mary were given the test in turn, and to the astonishment of the congregation they emerged from it triumphantly. Neither of them was affected in any way, no 'sign' appeared, and amid rejoicing and wonder their innocence from carnal sin was proclaimed. Here, to priest and people alike, the greater, the thaumaturgical wonder was revealed, the irreconcilable reconciled, and all Man's experience set aside by this great exception: Mary, the mother-to-be, had known not Joseph, had committed no adultery, had known no man. It was manifest to all that the child to come was of a very special nature: perhaps, even, Divine. And among the general rejoicing Mary and
36 Joseph returned to their house to await the momentous birth.

4 The birth of Jesus

. . . it came to pass in those days, that there went out a decree from Caesar Augustus, that all the world should be taxed.
(And this taxing was first made when Cyrenius was Governor of Syria.)
And all went to be taxed, every one into his own city.
And Joseph also went up from Galilee, out of the city of Nazareth, into Judaea, into the city of David, which is called Bethlehem (because he was of the house and lineage of David)
to be taxed with his espoused wife, being **great** *with child.*

Luke has always had it, as he does here, that Joseph and Mary lived in Nazareth, even though he makes Mary visit in improbably distant 'Juda', which argues his unfamiliarity with the Holy Land. And at this point in their narratives the apocryphal writers themselves, who have a predilection for a home in Bethlehem of Judea, switch to Galilee. This, then, meant that Joseph had to make a long journey south to his ancestral tribal centre near Jerusalem; and he had to take with him not only the girl Mary, his *espoused wife, being great with child*, but the wherewithal to pay the levy. It was for this reason that Joseph, who is here seen as no more than an itinerant carpenter, a poor man by definition, brought down with him his ox — which with the ass which Mary rode formed all his cattle — hoping that it would fetch a better price in nearby Jerusalem than in his own relatively poor and mountainous province of Galilee. So, to anticipate a little in our story, the apocryphal ox came to Bethlehem: and this was the ox which, with the ass, was to warm with its breath the infant Jesus, and this the ox which, in memory of that far-off time, we set in our cribs at Christmas.

The journey from Nazareth to Bethlehem was the first which Mary and Joseph had made together, and it must have been no easy undertaking. It was a long and hard road, with high ground for much of the way, and marshy tracks in the Decapolis and Perea, on that left bank of the Jordan which they would have had to have followed to avoid the uncertainties of Samaria. And there must have been many families travelling on the same route, returning to their native cities for the

67

taxing, so that it was not surprising in those exceptional circumstances that when they got to their journey's end, *there was no room at the inn.* But by now the need of the little party for shelter was imperative, for it was here and now, in Bethlehem itself, or in the fields about the town, that Luke tells us that *the days were accomplished that she should be* 9 37 39 43 *delivered* and that Mary *brought forth her first-born son, and wrapped him in swaddling clothes, and laid him in the manger.*

This is all that Luke has to say about the birth; and Matthew, who knew nothing of the Annunciation and the Visitation and the Taxing, shuffles off that climactic event in a single uneasy phrase. But from the major apocryphal texts—and particularly from the Protevangelium— we learn a great deal more of this day on which Jesus was born. To take the story from the beginning, we must go back along the road a little, to the hill country near Bethlehem; Mary was very young and for two weeks at least she had been travelling a difficult road on donkey-back, so that it is not surprising that towards the end of her journey she began to suffer from hallucinations and to see visions. On the last morning, on the day of the birth itself, she saw before her a band of people 'rejoicing and exulting', and others nearby 'weeping and lamenting'. She told Joseph at length of what she saw, and in later times these visions were

37 A narrative picture—the Annunciation; the doubting and suspicious Joseph is reconciled with Mary; and the birth of Jesus with Salome and the 'undefiled daughters of the Hebrews'. Mural in St Clement's, Ochrid, Yugoslavia, thirteenth century.

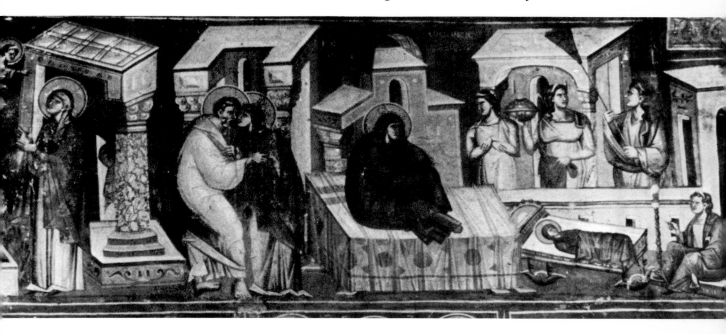

firmly believed to have been a happy premonition of the Gentiles rejoicing at the birth to come, and of the Jews weeping, for from this time they were destined to 'depart from their God'. But her husband, from whom these things were hidden, bade her not to waste her strength in idle words, and to sit her beast as best she might. And at last, when they were in the hills at the third milestone from Bethlehem, Mary knew that she could go no further. 'Take me down from the ass,' she said, 'for my time has come, and my burden urges to be delivered.' So Joseph lifted her down, and led her into an abandoned cave-house by the roadside, for they were halted in a wild and desolate spot which offered no better shelter for a girl in labour. Leaning against a pillar — perhaps a wooden roof-prop — within the cave, Mary gripped it tightly with her hands. But Joseph, the pious churchman and ritualist, feared the impurities of childbirth, in which men should have no part, and he left her alone in her extremity. Unsaddling the ass, he set out down the road, hoping that he would meet with some woman who would know about these things, and who would come to help his wife.

He had not gone far when a mysterious power halted him in his tracks, and he stood as one paralysed. He saw before him 'workmen by the roadside, holding drinking vessels, but their hands did not move. Those who had put cup to lip, their lips were still; but the faces of all were looking upward. The sheep were scattered in the field, but the sheep did not move. The shepherd had lifted his staff to strike, but the blow did not descend. The mouths of the kids were on the surface of the stream, but they did not drink.' Joseph could not yet know it, but in the cave behind him Jesus had been born. In that transcending moment, all the world stood still as if it held its breath.

The good man came to himself again, and was continuing his way when he saw a woman 'coming down from the hill country' whom he called to him, and, explaining his case, asked for help. This she was very willing to give, for by a happy chance she was a midwife by trade; and they hurried back along the road together. When they came near, Joseph was amazed to see that what had been little more than a dark and makeshift lodging in the cliffs at the roadside had become 'filled with a brilliant light, as bright as if it were in the fields at the sixth hour of the day'. And within, wonder of wonders, they found Mary, who had recently been in dire labour, filled with gentle pride, and seemingly in perfect health and composure. She was sitting on the saddle of the ass, and her new-born babe, naked, spotless and serene, lay quietly on the ground at her feet.

The midwife — Maia is thought to have been her name — felt uneasy, and was at first inclined to take Joseph to task for having wasted her time. But now, at last, Mary seemed herself to realise that

38 A Janus-headed Satan encourages Joseph to disbelieve the story of the virgin birth. Detail from a Byzantine altarpiece, fifteenth century.

she was indeed the medium through which unique events had come to pass, and she spoke up for herself, and told the midwife something of her tale. And in the Koran, indeed, the child himself speaks up, and forces belief. Such of the story as the woman could immediately grasp was more than a little difficult for her to accept; yet she felt herself to be in the presence of some extraordinary phenomenon, and very quickly

she 'believed' in the virginity of the mother and knew that so exceptional a child could not but be divine. And setting herself to what remained of her professional tasks, she bathed, from old habit, the spotless child, and wrapping him in his swaddling clothes and handing him into his mother's arms, she prostrated herself before them with humility and pride.

9   A little later—though, in the Byzantine tradition she arrives almost at the birth itself—a young woman called Salome, one of Maia's friends and neighbours, passed along the road. The midwife called out to her excitedly to come and see an extraordinary marvel: a child, a boy, divine, and born of a woman who had known no man. Salome mocked her, treating this dressing up of an old story with the scorn which it seemed to merit; but her curiosity, and a desire to gossip, made her come to the mouth of the cave to see what was going on. She talked with the midwife and Joseph, and laughed at their tale, saying that she could never believe the ridiculous story that a mother could be a virgin unless she had tactile proof of the fact and had examined the mother herself. Apparently, this bold suggestion was quite readily agreed to, for Maia said to Mary: 'Arrange yourself, as there is no little controversy about you'. Then, in the words of Pseudo-Matthew, 'Salome put out her hand. But when she withdrew her hand from examining her, her hand immediately withered and dried up.' She had found a virgin: and in pain, weeping and terrified, believing already in a great, a heaven-sent miracle, she called in contrition and fear on God to heal her and to pardon her lack of faith.

Her prayer was quickly answered, for 'there appeared a certain youth, who said to her, Approach the infant and adore him, and touch
44   the hem of his swaddling clothes with your hand, and he will make you whole . . . and adoring the child, she approached him, and touching the hem of his garment, immediately her hand was healed.' But, said the youth—in the Protevangelian version of the tale—'tell not of the strange things which you have seen until the child shall enter Jerusalem.' Salome, overcome with wonder, overwhelmed by the miracle and the apparition, fell to the ground and swore that from that moment, and quitting all else, she would truly serve the virgin mother and her child, and never leave them for the rest of her life.

39 Scenes from the life of Mary: the Annunciation, the Visitation, the Birth of Jesus, and the Three Kings. From the Altenberg Altarpiece, German, *c.* 1350.

5 The first days of Jesus

And there were in the same country shepherds abiding in the fields, keeping watch over their flock by night.

And lo!, the angel of the Lord came upon them, and the glory of the Lord shone round them, and they were sore afraid.

40

For the angel said unto them, Fear not: for behold, I bring you tidings of great joy, which shall be to all people.

For unto you is born this day, in the city of David, a Saviour, which is Christ the Lord.

And this shall be a sign unto you: Ye shall find the babe wrapped in swaddling clothes, lying in a manger.

And suddenly there was with the angel a multitude of the heavenly host, praising God, and saying,

Glory to God in the highest, and on earth peace, good will towards men.

And it came to pass, as the angels were gone away from them into Heaven, the shepherds said to one another, Let us now go even unto Bethlehem, and see this thing which is come to pass, which the Lord hath made known us.

And they came with haste, and found Mary, and Joseph, and the babe lying in a manger.

And when they had seen it, they made known abroad the saying which was told them concerning this child.

And all they that heard it wondered at those things which were told them by the shepherds.

But Mary kept all these things, and pondered them in her heart.

As a story, as a striking incident of the 'Birth' period, this 'Annunciation to the Shepherds' can be compared only with Matthew's tale of the Magi and Herod. It contrasts curiously, in its length and relative completeness, with the verse of Luke, and the brief phrase of Matthew, which is all that the Evangelists devote to the birth itself. We should, then, look in some detail at these shepherds, and at the treatment of their tale in Christian art.

40 The Annunciation to the Shepherds. From a French Book of Hours, 1440–50.

From the point of view of urban societies, and until modern times, shepherds were the solitaries, even the wild men, of the hills. They were seldom seen in towns, and were generally unwelcome there, particularly if they came at night, and without their flocks, as these men must have done. In the structured and civilised Roman world of which Syrian Judea, in New Testament times, had for two generations formed a part, these 'abominations to the Egyptians' were the outsiders, despised and sometimes feared, who lived beyond the pale: and they would have stank, as all working shepherds stank until the invention of modern sheep-dips.

Normally, in the brief but sometimes sharp winters of Syria, the sheep and goats would have been folded in a sheltered valley, and what these particular herdsmen were doing with their flocks on the open hillside in the bitter cold nights of a Palestine December is open to question; but Luke's story has it that they had been out there in the 'field', the solitary places, that they had been given a dazzling celestial display, and that the angels had brought to them the stupendous news that in the city of David, the city of Bethlehem, had been born a Saviour, the Redeemer for which the whole Jewish nation had been waiting for generations. They may not entirely have believed that they could have been the chosen vessels for so momentous a disclosure; they may have feared some urban trick. But, breaking all the rules, they left their flocks, and when they had found the child in the manger, and had seen the scene with their own eyes — and perhaps heard Salome's story from her own lips — they believed that an extraordinary event had happened and that they of all people had been forewarned of it. They did not, as far as we know, make any immediate comment; and instead of staying at this memorable scene, they went to bruit their news abroad, and we hear no more of them.

Their visit had been brief, cursory, laconic. And Luke's shepherds did not 'worship', as did the Magi of Matthew. The distinction is a curious one, and infrequently observed by the world at large, though it is generally well taken in the familiar representations of the scene. We should compare the behaviour of these men with the Magi, who, when they 'were come into the house, saw the young child with Mary his mother, and fell down, and worshipped him': that is to say, they prostrated themselves in the oriental fashion, with palms and forehead to the ground. Now it took many centuries for these Magi to develop, in the popular imagination, into kings. By the time that their crowns had become firmly set on their heads, and the Magi, the eastern astronomers, forgotten, all Europe was feudal; every man, in an unbroken chain from prince to cottar, owed homage and duties to his superior, and at least once in his life bent the knee to him in an individual act of submission.

So, in the endless mediaeval pictures of the 'Adoration of the Kings', we are accustomed to see the eldest of these apocryphal monarchs, not perhaps 'falling down', but in the manner of the time going down on bended knee, offering his propitiatory gifts to a greater king than he; while behind him stand his younger peers, respectfully waiting their turn to make their separate and personal genuflection.

The shepherds are almost never shown performing this act, and they seldom bend the knee in direct and personal homage to their new-found Lord. Nor do they prostrate themselves. They are usually depicted standing, perhaps leaning on their staves, or squatting on their heels, and viewing the scene before them with unsmiling detachment. It may have been in this way that the manner of the painting of them had been laid down in the earliest pattern books; and in late mediaeval times, and on into the Renaissance, this treatment, which echoes accurately the words of Luke, had become a firm visual tradition. It is curious to reflect that this mis-called 'Adoration of the Shepherds' is virtually the only subject-representation — save certain Crucifixions — in the whole of Christian art which translates into pictorial form with reasonable accuracy what the New Testament actually says.

In passing, it is interesting to take a look at pictures of the shepherds' staves: it will be seen that the working end of these is not in any sense the leg- or neck-crook which is generally thought of as the shepherd's tool, but resembles a small shovel, or, sometimes, a soup spoon. Many shepherds carried simple staves or clubs; but the shovels are in fact hurling-tools: when a browsing sheep strayed too far from its fellows, it was not always advisable to send a dog to round it up, for too many sheep might be disturbed in the operation and the grazing pattern broken up unnecessarily. The shepherd, then, would dig up a clod of earth — or pick up a stone — with his 'spade' or spoon, and hurl it, with an aim born of long practice, to land just beyond the wandering animal; which, startled, would shy back towards its fellows. This was the standard tool, and standard practice, throughout Europe, as an examination of most 'Adorations of the Shepherds' will show, and any form of hooked staff was exceedingly rare. Even when the French court at Versailles played at shepherds and shepherdesses, the fragile staffs of the courtiers had shovel ends, as a closer look at the pictures of Watteau and Lancret will confirm. The Bishop's crozier has no common origin with the shepherd's staff; and the metallic crook which we associate with the shepherd of today, and which is infallibly seen in modern religious pictures in the hands of Christ-the-guardian-of-his-flock, is a product of the Industrial Revolution.

But to return to our story: after their disturbed night with the visiting herdsmen, the little family spent the next six days in their cave,

44 45

or in the adjoining one, where there was a manger which made a safe and convenient cradle for the child. We know of only one major incident which happened during this time, which has no known apocryphal source, but which has been abundantly attested to throughout Christian history. We learn of a calamity, relieved by a major miracle. On the third day, Mary's milk dried up, and she could no longer feed her babe. According to the story told to pilgrims, he almost died of hunger; but Mary's agonised prayers were eventually answered in so spectacular a fashion that her breasts suddenly swelled to bursting, and the milk streamed from them with such force that not only was Jesus able to drink abundantly, but the floor and even the walls of the cave were spattered and whitened by the generous flood. This singular happening was destined to be remembered until quite modern times as a great miracle, and one particularly cherished by the womenkind of Christendom, and even of Islam; so that the wonder-working 'Cave of the Milk of the Virgin' was transferred in mediaeval times to Jerusalem and became one of the chief tourist attractions and one of the principal shrines of the Holy Land. Throughout the centuries, from the first recorded visit by the 'Bordeaux Pilgrim' in the year 333, traveller after traveller, pilgrim after pilgrim, visited this miraculous grotto and left us their description of it.

The Crusaders, during the brief century when they held Jerusalem, were familiar with the place; and later, in 1375, Simon de Salebruche, Baron d'Anglure, found that within the famous cave there was still the pillar — but now of marble — against which the Virgin had braced herself when her time had come. In his day, it had become one of the 'sweating stones' which exuded moisture, and of which there were several in the Holy Places, each, like the 'Pillar of the Scourging', marking the site of an ancient and sacred pain. de Salebruche's 'Grotte du Lait de la Vierge' had become the crypt of a church dedicated to St Nicholas, and to explain the location, and to make the hallowed ground still more remarkable, it was held that the miracle had taken place on this spot while the Virgin and her child were hiding from Herod's troops. It was already an ancient article of faith that a pinch of dust from the walls or floor of the cave, taken with a little water, was an infallible cure against deficient lactation, and so much had been

opposite
41 The Visitation: a mingling of the styles of the East and the West. Mural in the Latin Chapel in the monastery church of St John Lampadistis, Kalapanayiotis, Cyprus.

overleaf
42 Mary undergoes the Trial by the Water of the Conviction of the Lord which will establish her blamelessness. Mural in the church of St Sozomenus, Galata, Cyprus.

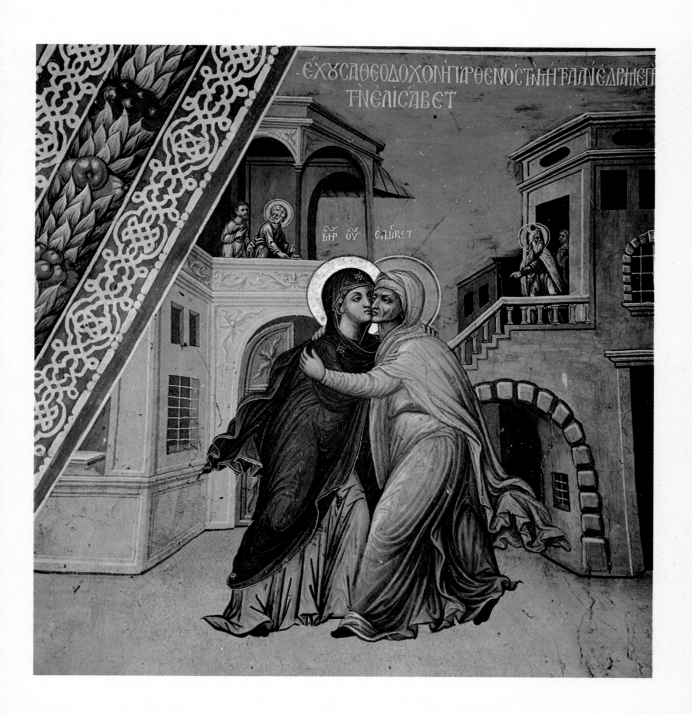

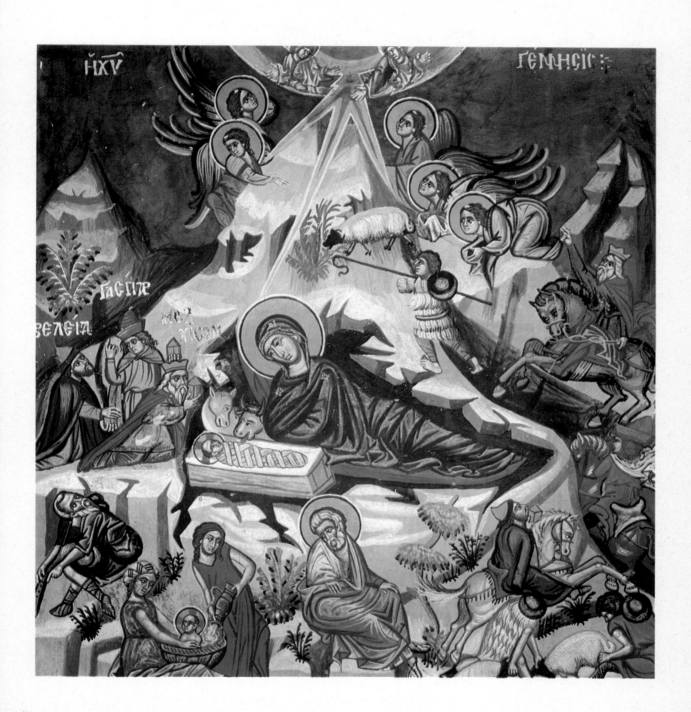

purchased by pilgrims from the resident clergy that the cave had become enormously enlarged, though the floor and the walls were still as white as ever.

This therapeutic tradition lasted until at least the beginning of the seventeenth century, for the Protestant William Lithgow, a careful but loquacious Scot who had visited the cave, recounts the story of the miracle in his 'Rare Adventures and Painefull Peregrinations' of 1632, and says that the dust was available not only 'to Christians, but likewise to Turkish, Moorish, and Arabianish women, who will come from far countries to fetch of this earth. I have seen the nature of this dust practised, wherefore I may boldly affirm it to have a strange virtue. Of which earth I brought with me a pound weight, and presented the half of it to our sometime gracious Queen Anne [of Denmark, wife of James I] of blessed memory, with divers other relics also, as a girdle, and a pair of garters of the Holy Grave, all richly wrought in silk and gold . . .'

This commercialisation of the Holy Places by their guardian churches has gone on throughout Christian history; but the arch-dissenter Calvin was surely overstating the case when he wrote that there was hardly a Catholic church or monastery in Switzerland, however small, which did not possess a 'relic' of the Virgin's milk, and added, with characteristic savagery, that had she been a milch cow or a wet nurse all her life, she would have been hard put to it to produce so great a quantity. Unfortunately no picture of this famous cave appears to have survived.

This singular story of the 'milk' is the only one we know of from those first days; but on the sixth day after the birth, says Pseudo-Matthew, the little party changed their quarters and spent that night and the succeeding day, the eve of the ritual circumcision and name giving ceremony, in Bethlehem itself. Luke's Gospel records that 47 *when eight days were accomplished for the circumcising of the child, his name was called JESUS, which was so named of the angel before he was conceived in the womb.* 'Jesus', signifying 'Saviour', was one of the more popular Jewish names of the time: Flavius Josephus wrote of several

overleaf
43 In this Byzantine compendium or narrative picture Jesus is shown in his cot, and being bathed by Salome and Maia. The Three Kings are shown on their journey, and at their arrival; and the shepherds are also present. Mural by Philip Goul in the Church of the Holy Cross, Platanistasa, Cyprus, fifteenth century.

opposite
44 A nativity with the shepherds: Salome, standing on the right, is displaying her hand, which is no longer withered, and the phylactery tells us that she 'believes because she has touched'. By the Master of Flemalle, fifteenth century.

45 The shepherds bringing gifts: note the staff on the ground. Engraving by Giorgio Ghisi after Bronzino, sixteenth century.

men so called, and in the fifties of the first century two successive High Priests of the Temple of Jerusalem bore the name; they were both almost certainly near-contemporaries, but not relatives, of our own Jesus.

The ritual of circumcision and name-giving made up the act of admission to the Jewish religion, as baptism does for the Christian church, and neither the barn of Luke nor the cave of the apocryphals would have been considered a proper place for so solemn a ceremony. We can assume, then, that the tradition of Pseudo-Matthew is correct and that the ceremony took place in Bethlehem, probably in the priest's house; but none of our sources give details of the work of that day. Perhaps because of this, the matter has been handled in artifacts in many different ways, and sometimes painters have become confused in their chronology and show Salome carrying the two turtle doves which properly belong to the 'Presentation'. Moreover the delicate nature of the operation was sometimes forgotten, or misunderstood, for we often see the priest wielding a weapon quite inappropriate to the work in hand.

The physical ritual of the circumcision, however, gave rise to one tradition of the solidest kind, which spread throughout the Christian world and which has persisted almost to our own day: it was said that after the operation Salome, who was by now confirmed in her worship of the child, managed to secure for herself the prepuce, that tiny morsel of severed flesh. Her brother was a perfumer — or, as some apocryphals said, a barber — who would have had all sorts of preservative materials in his stock-in-trade; and she thought well to confide the precious object to him and he put it up in a jar of spikenard. A late tradition had it that this was the oil of spikenard which the Mary of the Gospel of John poured over the feet of Jesus. But according to the so-called 'Arabic' Gospel of the Infancy, which suggests that Jesus' umbilical cord had already been preserved in something of the same way — though to our knowledge it has never been heard of since — Salome had told her brother never to part with it, even though he were to be offered so great a sum as 300 dinars for its possession.

But eventually, by some remarkable alchemy, this exceptional relic, the only corporeal particle of Jesus remaining on the face of the earth, was so greatly multiplied that it became an object of simultaneous veneration at Besançon, at le Puy, at the Abbey of Charroux, and at Chartres, where the particularly sacred object was held to have been given to Charlemagne in Jerusalem itself, and to have been brought by him to Paris, and then to Poitiers, and eventually to its home in the great cathedral. It was a mighty relic in Antwerp and in Bruges, in Nancy, Metz and Hildesheim; and at Calcutta, where it lay in its reliquary near to the tomb of St Thomas, the evangelist of India. Of course it was present at Rome, where there seem at one time to have been two separate examples in churches at different ends of the town, and where perhaps most remarkably, it was still, according to Harris Cowper, being exposed in a church—almost certainly St John Lateran—in the 1890s. There have been, of course, dissident views. Some Jesuit theologians held that Christ rose from the dead with the prepuce intact and the whole body perfect; and St Catherine of Siena believed that the tiny ring of flesh was that with which Jesus was to wed all mankind. But today, in what are perhaps more enlightened times, and in all the sites where once it worked miracles or brought solace, all knowledge of its physical presence is denied.

The circumcision took place on the eighth day of Jesus' life, and it is customary to believe that it was four days later, on the twelfth day, that he received the visit of the 'Three Kings', and that it was on twelfth night, the Epiphany, that they slept in Bethlehem and *being warned of God in a dream that they should not return to Herod, they departed into their countries by another way.* Now these men, the Magi, the Kings, warned by a *star in the east* which we assume without biblical authority to have marked the moment of Jesus' birth, had already made the journey to Jerusalem and had been at the court of Herod; and they had come from 'the East', which was a generic term for a far-off country beyond man's ken. 'How, then,' said these men of the middle ages, with their pragmatic minds, 'could they have made so great a journey in so short a time?' The answer which was sometimes advanced was that they had been borne on strange beasts called dromedaries, and that it was well known that dromedaries travelled unwearyingly at three, or six, or even ten times the speed of horses.

In the Miracle Plays, where some sort of unity of time is observed, the kings make their apperance hot-foot upon the birth scenes, and in time to be in Bethlehem for Twelfth Night. But prudent men followed the tradition which had come down from the Gospel of Pseudo-Matthew, which has them arriving in Judea two years after the birth of Jesus, when he, of course, was just two years old; which in turn makes it less irrational for 'Herod the King' to have ordered, as a consequence of their visit, the masacre of 'all the children that were in Bethlehem, and in the coasts thereof, from two years old and under'.

This 'Herod the King', was Herod the Great, one of the greatest men of the ancient world; soldier, orator, statesman, and an intimate and trusted friend of the Emperor Augustus for almost thirty years. His half-share of the enormously rich copper mines of Cyprus, together with the provinces of Syria and Palestine which he ruled over as client-king, made him the wealthiest man in the Empire; and he lavished his fortune in so prodigal a fashion for his own vain glory, and in celebration of the Emperor, and for the goodwill of the people, that it is said that in all the history of Rome only Hadrian built more monuments and temples and public buildings than he. He is one of the best attested characters of his times, yet his vital dates appear seriously to confuse our accepted chronology, for he died, by then an antique tyrant, in 4 B.C. But of course, he died after the birth of Jesus, after he had seen the Magi, after their escape. Nevertheless this apparent anomaly is not so unsettling as it would appear to be, for our protagonist was born, as far as his contemporaries were concerned, in the year 39 or 40 of the Julian calendar of the Roman world of his time. Our own, the Christian calendar, was invented in about the year 550 by a Scythian monk with the curious name of Dionysius Exiguus. He worked backwards through the centuries from his own time to the zero moment of the birth of Jesus, that dividing line between 'B.C.' and 'A.D.'; and though the texts from which he drew his calculations were often confusing and contradictory he got that moment in time right to within, say, six or seven years, or about one per cent of an intervening period which was as long as that which separates us from the battle of Agincourt.

He undershot the mark by those few years, but it was a remarkable performance, and allows us to accept with confidence the chronology implicit in Matthew's Gospel, and to set the birth of Jesus, in our accepted notation, at the end of the year 7 B.C. Apocryphal chronology also supports this date, and we have to assume that in the two years which followed, the first two years of Jesus's life, the astonishing miracle of his birth and the strange events which surrounded it became nine days' wonders, quickly forgotten by the world at large. The family would have lived on quietly in Bethlehem, with Joseph going about his carpenter's tasks. And then, at the winter solstice of 5 B.C., came these Wise Men, the 'Magi', from the East.

6 The Three Kings and the Presentation

The Bible does not speak of 'Kings', and does not tell us how many 'wise men' came to Bethlehem. Persians held that there were no less than twelve of them, bringing gold, and myrrh, and frankincense, and they tell us their names, and the names of their fathers. But from very early times, in a Syrian tradition recorded in the 'Book of the Cave of Treasures' of perhaps the sixth century, the number of them was three, the magic number, the number of the Trinity, and they were already Kings: the King of Persia, King of Kings; the King of Saba; and the King of Sheba in the East. According to Solomon of Bassorah, they came to Judea with so great a following that 'cities were afraid, and closed their gates', and Herod in Jerusalem, with superstitious fear, said that if this child they sought was so mighty that he could even require tribute from the Persians, he himself would go and fall at his feet: though evil was in his heart, and he still plotted to kill him and so to become the 'King of all the World'.

In these Syrian texts the great personages of a later day, who became the Kings Caspar, and Melchior, and Balthasar, are beginning to emerge, and in parts of Byzantium, and even as far west as Ravenna, the trio—for this significant number was early accepted—appears occasionally as kings in relatively early Christian times. To Tertullian they were indeed 'fere reges', or almost kings, in the year 200, but in the artifacts of the west, for 1,000 years, they remained Magi, astronomers and men of magic, and in place of the crowns which they were later to assume they usually wore the Phrygian cap which in mediaeval times denoted the Jew, and which reappeared as the 'Cap of Liberty' in the French Revolution. Until about the twelfth century the three are uniform, without distinguishing marks or dress. Then, when they had become established in the popular imagination as kings, they assume royal regalia and begin to be more sharply differentiated as the old, the younger and the young king, symbolic of the three ages of manhood and of the lifetime of devotion which was owed to the King of Kings; and, as symbols of universal worship, they came to represent the three parts of the known world—Europe, Asia, and Africa. In the early Middle Ages these continents were most often thought of in terms of their Mediterranean lands, and as the pigmentation of the inhabitants of all the shores of the inland sea varied little, and was thought of as being white, all the kings were 'white'. It was only when the Portuguese voyages of the fourteenth century had begun to show the true size of Africa, and the blackness of its inhabitants, that it became necessary that one of them, in the interest of universality, should represent that great continent at the 'Adoration', and that the notion of a 'Black King' was born. By a natural extension of this concept we even find on occasions, in the art of Spain and Portugal of two centuries later, a worshipping king from the New World, with a dark skin and decked out in what was imagined as Incan or Peruvian dress.

But in their first beginnings in that far-off time these three Magi, these three 'Kings', guided, we are told, by the same star, met in a desert place—or, as Maundeville says with his suspect precision, 'In a city in Ind, that men call Cassak, that is a 53 days' journey from Bethlehem'—and travelled together to Jerusalem. There they asked, publicly and with un-oriental directness: Where was the child who was to be King of the Jews? It was an explosive question. King Herod

46 The Kings riding to Jerusalem. From a fourteenth century Italian manuscript.

the Great was King of the Jews. He had been so for forty years past, and he saw himself as founder of a dynasty, with his sons and grandsons as his successors; so that it was no wonder that 'he was troubled, and all Jerusalem with him'. But now Herod was in his last days, old, sick to death, and intermittently insane, and in the superstitious fears of his fevered mind it seemed essential to him to find this child and to suppress him out of hand. But the Magi did not yet know where he was to be found, so — in Matthew's Gospel — the *chief priests and scribes of the people*, which in this context means the full Sanhedrin of the Sadducean hierarchy and the Pharisean scribes, were called together to consult the scriptures, which, though the science of typology was not yet born, were the source of universal prediction: and they quite easily found the answer in the fifth chapter of the Book of Micah. Bethlehem was the place: *But thou, Bethlehem Ephratah, though thou be little among the thousands of Judah, yet out of thee shall he come forth unto me that is to be ruler in Israel; whose going forth have been from of old, from everlasting.*

51 This seemed conclusive. But Herod thereupon issued the extraordinary order for the Magi to go to Bethlehem, apparently without any escort of his own men, or any supervision, and for them to come back to him when they found the child so that, as he said in his senile cunning, he could follow in their tracks and *worship him also*. The Magi, then, went on their way, and helped by the same star as they

4 50 had seen in their homeland, they found the young child Jesus. Accepting his special character without any hesitation, they gave him, on bended knee, their propitiatory and well chosen gifts: gold to relieve poverty; frankincense against the smell of the stable; and myrrh to put away vermin. Or, as the Syrians had it, 'gold for a king, frankincense for a priest, myrrh for a physician. For he was a king, a priest, and a physician'. Some eastern traditions have it that they were rewarded with a piece of the child's clothing, and that they eventually carried this precious relic back with them to their homeland, where it burnt eternally as one of the Zoroastrian fires of divination. But on this day, when they had done their duties to the child, they retired to the inn, and that night, warned in a dream — presumably by a member of their

opposite
47 The Circumcision, with Joseph himself carrying the two young pigeons of the Presentation. By Andrea Mantegna, fifteenth century.

overleaf
48 The Three Kings, guided by the star, have met and will begin their journey to Jerusalem. From the Poor Man's Bible window in Canterbury Cathedral, thirteenth century.

own pantheon—that they should not return to Herod, they left by
another way and, it was said, took ship in haste in the harbour of
Tarshish and sailed away to the East.

These wise men, it seems, had been Herod's only means of identify-
ing the child precisely, and it was once believed that when he received the news that they had slipped out of his hands, he was
convulsed with anger and had his ailing body carried to the port in
pursuit. But, of course, he arrived too late. In one of the insane rages
to which he had long been subject, he is said to have ordered every
ship in Tarshish harbour to be burnt to the waterline, and their crews
strung up; and then, returning to Jerusalem filled with superstitious
forebodings, he resolved to settle the matter once and for all and to
protect the inheritance of his sons by the wholesale massacre of every
suspect child. The township where they were to be found had been
located for him by the priests of the Temple, and perhaps remembering
rumours of a strange birth in the area a year or two before, he *sent
forth*—in Matthew's words—*and slew all the children that were in
Bethlehem . . . from two years old and under.* It was the 'Massacre of the
Innocents', preceded—but only just, for it was a close-run thing—by
the angelic warning which came to Joseph and which caused him,
before the arrival of Herod's troops, to flee from Herod's dominions to
the south, to Egypt, with his wife and the little child called Jesus.

The Magi themselves sailed away to the East, and came to India,
where they met St Thomas, who created them bishops and gave them
dioceses to rule which were more precious to them than their observatories
or their kingdoms. In due course, the eldest one died, and was buried
with great pomp in a splendid mausoleum. When the time came for
the second one to follow him, the first sat up in his tomb and moved
across to leave him room; and eventually the second moved across for
the body of the youngest, so that the three Kings-Magi-Bishops lay in
death together. Their Christian followers carried their bodies a great
journey over mountains and deserts, and re-buried them in their
Arabian homeland where, some three centuries later, the Dowager-

overleaf
49 In the distant Goreme valley of Cappadocia, the Wise Men, even in the thirteenth
century, had not yet become Kings in popular belief. Mural in the rock-cut church of
Karanlik Kilise, Turkey.

opposite
50 The Adoration of the Kings, who here represent the three ages of man, and the
three continents, Europe, Asia, and the Black Africa which the Portuguese navigators
had discovered. Panel from the Adoration Triptych, by the 'Master of the Bob Jones
University Adoration'.

51 The Magi before Herod. By Matteo di Giovanni, School of Siena, 1430–95.

Empress Helena of Constantinople lighted upon them, in something of the same manner as she had, with the most remarkable good fortune, discovered the wood of the True Cross, and had their bodies disinterred.

She took them home, and for more than 800 years they had an honourable place among the multitude of relics which lay in the Byzantine capital; but in 1150, Constantine Paleologus, Emperor of the East, a man careless in the magnificence of his gifts, made a present of the remains to Eustorgius the Archbishop of Milan, who had a special ship and special carriages made to carry them back in triumph to his own cathedral. They were not suffered to stay in their new home for long. Twelve years later Frederick Barbarossa captured the city, sacked it with great thoroughness, and carried off the bodies of the 'Three Kings' as booty. He had them sent back to his own capital, Cologne, where the extraordinary sanctity of these relics, and the pilgrims and the gift-offerings in money and lands and treasure which they attracted through all the following centuries, made the single most important contribution to the building and the re-building of the great cathedral, to the revenues of its clergy, and to the prosperity of the town. And there, in the 'City of the Three Kings', in the cathedral of Cologne, the bemused visitor of today may still bow the knee before the gorgeous reliquary which contains the travel-worn remains of these three old Magi of another world, and drop his obole in the box which stands beside them.

But to return to Bethlehem, and our story: on the eighth day the little child had been named Jesus, and circumcised according to the law. On the fortieth day, Joseph and Mary *when the days of her purification . . . were accomplished . . . brought him to Jerusalem, to present him to the Lord . . . and to offer a sacrifice according to that which is said in the law of the Lord, A pair of turtle doves, or two young pigeons.* By this fortieth day, Mary was considered as cleansed from the inescapable impurities of childbirth and could again be admitted to a place of worship; and Joseph, who in the words of Matthew *knew her not till she had brought forth her firstborn son,* was presumably released from the 'trust' which had been imposed upon him. This was the day when the law required that the infant be brought to the Temple, or to the local place of worship, for his 'Presentation to the Lord' and his dedication to the Jewish faith and nation; and at this ceremony the parents were required to make a gift to the officiating clergy of animals or birds of certain kinds—and ideally of a certain age and condition—which were ritually slaughtered and blooded, and the bodies tendered to the altar fires as 'burnt offerings' to the Lord. Afterwards, the partly charred flesh became the perquisite of the priests for their table; and the whole occasion was a festival at which rich Jews made splendid offerings. We can, for example, reasonably suppose that a few months before the birth of Jesus, herds of cattle and sheep and goats would have been driven into the forecourt of the Temple by the servants of Zacharias and Elizabeth when, on their own 'fortieth day', they came for the joyful Presentation of their late-born only son.

But Joseph was a poor man, and could afford but the least of the offerings which was acceptable under the law: the *pair of turtle doves, or two young pigeons.* These he would almost certainly have bought in the Temple itself from the tradesmen who sold Presentation offerings of every kind; just as, at the Passover, when Jews from many lands were gathered home to Jerusalem, money-changers, at their tables in the court of the Temple, would convert into shekels and beka and gera the foreign coins which the pilgrims would have brought with them for their journey and their offerings. A generation later, too many of these merchants may have invaded the sacred precincts, for it was then that Jesus when the *Passover was at hand . . . found in the Temple those that sold oxen and sheep and doves, and the changers of money sitting: And when he had made a scourge of small cords, he drove them out. . . .* These men, these merchants, performed a public service and were at least tolerated, if not encouraged, by the clergy; but Jesus was never tender to the Establishment, and quick to anger.

So Joseph bought his pair of pigeons, with just that sheen on the neck feathers which was called for by the law; and hundreds of artifacts show us the scene, sometimes with Salome carrying the birds in a little wicker basket, or nestling them in her arms. And sometimes, at this greatest of all Presentations, we see an aged man, perhaps standing a little apart from the central group, or, sometimes, even holding the infant Jesus in his arms. This is old Simeon, who was *waiting for the consolation of Israel: and the Holy Ghost was upon him.* A strange story—the origins of which we do not know—is told of this man, which takes us to the great library of the Ptolomies at Alexandria, where it is known that there were Greek versions of the Old Testament; and which builds on this historic fact a curious tissue of fancy in which, perhaps, some truth is embedded. Luke knew at least something of the tale, for he says of Simeon that, *It was revealed unto him by the Holy Ghost, that he should not see death before he had seen the Lord's Christ.*

It was said that the Macedonian, Ptolomy Philadelphus, who reigned over Egypt for almost forty years at the beginning of the third century B.C., and whose benefactions made the library of Alexandria the greatest in the world, was anxious to obtain a Greek translation of the sacred books of the Hebrews. None existed in the world at the time; and he sent a splendid embassy to the High Priest of Jerusalem with the request that he should send, at Ptolomy's expense, Jewish scholars learned in the Greek tongue to the library at Alexandria, there to execute the translation which he required. The High Priest was flattered and pleased, and himself led a party of seventy-two Hebrew-Greek scholars—six from each of the tribes of Israel—to Egypt.

It was decided that each man, as his particular task, should translate a book, or part of a book, of what we now call the 'Old' Testament. Lots were cast, and to Simeon, who was of the party, fell the first part of Isaiah. When his work had progressed as far as Chapter VII, v.14, which the Authorised Version renders as:

> *Behold, a virgin shall conceive, and bear a son, and you shall call his name Immanuel*

he hesitated. 'Surely,' he thought, 'if I translate the passage as it stands, the Egyptians will think that we Jews are credulous fools, and our sacred books unworthy of the attention of cultivated men.' He decided, then, to change the word 'virgin' into the more reasonable rendering: 'young woman'. As he prepared to write the words, his elbow seemed to be jogged, and his pen scratched the papyrus. He began to write again, and this time his right hand became paralysed. Turning round, he saw behind him a wrathful angel, who said to him, 'You, Simeon, have dared to doubt the word of God, and the prophecy which God has given you. For this crime, I sentence you to Life; and you shall not quit this world until you have seen with your own eyes the fulfilment of God's word.'

When the work was finished, the group returned home, laden with gifts. Time passed, and Simeon became old, and older still; and for generation after generation he dragged himself about in the Temple precincts, waiting for death, for the release which never came. But then, one day, a little child, with his mother Mary, and Joseph, was brought into the court of the Tabernacle: and Simeon knew that his deliverance had come. Taking the child to him, he cried out those famous words which we intone with, perhaps, insufficient attention to their meaning:

> *Lord! now lettest thou thy servant depart in peace, according to thy word:*
> *For mine eyes have seen they salvation, which thou hast prepared before the face of all people.*
> *To be a light to lighten the Gentiles,*
> *and the glory of thy people Israel.*

Jesus the Saviour was come. The aspirations of the Jewish race were to be accomplished and ancient prophecy fulfilled. Old Simeon could go home at last to death.

7 The flights from Bethlehem

Influenced by the Christmas cribs of today, and by the telescoping of the action in Christmas pageants, we tend to think that the birth of Jesus and the visit of the Magi happened within a single twelve-day period. But the Anglo-Saxon Chronicle and a few of the more ancient texts—whose influence lingered long in some outlying Christian lands—tell us that the 'astrologers' came to perform their act of homage when the child was a little more than one year old. However, we have seen that there are sound traditional and even biblical reasons for accepting a two-year gap between the birth and the arrival of the wise men from the East; and this is the view supported by some of the early and by most of the later mediaeval texts, some of whose authors even specify that the Magi had given their gifts to Jesus when he was exactly two years and twelve days old: the day of Twelfth Night, the memory of which is still with us. Even today, in Roman Catholic countries, the twelfth day of Christmas is the 'day of the Kings' when, as for example in France, every baker sells big cartwheel almond pastries, within which is hidden a bean—that ancient charm—which entitles its finder to be King for the day and to wear the tinsel crown which the baker gives with every cake.

The mediaeval stories had it that the Magi, who were by now of course the 'Three Kings', had each observed, and understood, the guiding star and that they had joined forces on the borders of their distant kingdoms on Jesus' second birthday, the 25th December: a day which, from the fourth century, and after a good deal of chopping and changing, had been chosen in order that the celebration of that great event might compete with, or amplify, the pagan festival of the winter solstice. We must accept that the next fourteen days had been sufficient for them to perform, on their swift dromedaries, the long journey to Jerusalem, to question and alarm the local Establishment, and to have their interview with Herod. From Jerusalem to Bethlehem was but a step. And there they would have found not an infant but a well-grown child sitting on his mother's knee, interested—but not surprised—by their arrival and perhaps, as they bow the knee before him, gravely accepting their gifts with his own hands. Mediaeval and Renaissance painters were quite clear on this point: the shepherds contemplate a new-born babe; the Kings, with few exceptions to the rule, worship a child.

It is not without importance that Jesus should have been at least two years old when the Magi alerted Herod to his danger and set in motion the events which led to the escape from Bethlehem and the

52 The urgency of the flight from Herod's brutal troops. By Nicholas Poussin, seventeenth century.

flight to Egypt. We ourselves have forgotten all that happened on that long and hard journey to the south, but mediaeval man knew it all. He would readily have believed, if he had been told so, that all the miracles and remarkable actions which the child performed on the way to Egypt had been the work of a babe in arms, because that babe was Jesus; but it was more convenient to know that he was already a young child, with the normal development—and in his case, far more than the normal development—which an age of between two and three years implies. A very few mediaeval painters who may have been tributary to the ancient 'one-year-old' tradition still show Mary carrying her child to Egypt in swaddling clothes; but many more show an older child who can look about him with perception and who would have walked and talked, and often does so in their pictures. When the angel of the Lord appeared to Joseph for the second time and warned him to depart, for Herod sought the *young child*—and not a babe— to destroy him, we should imagine that this child would have been able, when the party had hastily loaded up, to walk out to the donkey himself and be lifted to its crupper. Once this point is accepted, the events of this and later chapters can be scrutinised with a readier suspension of disbelief.

They left Bethlehem at night. After the divine warning of danger which had come to Joseph in his sleep, he had not hesitated for a moment. The painter's view was that he filled his travelling wallet with some rough provisions such as pilgrims might take for their day's food, and mounting Mary and her child on the ass he set out in the darkness, 52 hoping to put a few miles between him and Bethlehem before first light. In endless pictures of the 'Flight'—which after the birth and the crucifixion, and perhaps the 'Three Kings', is the most popular subject in Christian art—they are shown as travelling in this way, without encumbrances, and with the wallet often slung over Joseph's staff. Some held that the ox from Nazareth, which it had not yet been necessary to sell to pay the tribute, went with them; and sometimes a 54 64 more prudent Joseph is shown taking with him into exile the tools of his carpenter's trade. One of the versions of the 'Gospels of Thomas' upgrades their social status, and makes them stockmasters who with their servants drove the family flocks and herds before them in their

opposite
53 The Kings *warned of God in a dream that they should not return to Herod ... departed ... another way,* here by sea from Tarshish. From a twelfth century German manuscript.

overleaf
54 The Presentation of Jesus to the Temple, and the release of old Simeon: Anne, the woman nearest to the child, is in Carmelite habit. By Quentin Metsys, 1466–1530.

flight. Had they had such flocks, and done this, their march would have been slowed beyond reason, and this improbable invention can have no basis in fact: no more indeed than a curious Coptic tradition that Herod himself—a man sick to death at the time—had directed the search in Bethlehem, and that when he had discovered that those whom he sought had fled southwards a few hours before, he set out after them with a troop of cavalry. In his rage, and his superstitious terror that his prey might escape him, he outdistanced his own men, and when eventually he saw the group before him he galloped over the plain towards them, brandishing his sword. But when he was almost upon them, divine intervention gave his horse such a fall that he was thrown to the ground and stunned, and the little party escaped over the hills before the arrival of his troops.

Their escape, in any case, was a close-run thing. It would have taken Joseph and his party at least four days to escape from immediate danger and to cross the border, some seventy or eighty miles away, into country where Herod's writ no longer ran. On this first morning, they were not yet many miles from Bethlehem and they must have known that their flight would have been discovered and that Herod's troops were on their trail. It seemed that the slow-moving little group, plodding on at a donkey's pace, would be overtaken at any moment; but divine assistance and an ingenious stratagem saved them *in extremis*. Pressing onwards, they passed by a field where there were some peasants sowing wheat, and Mary said to them: 'If Herod's men come this way and ask if you have seen a party such as ours, you must say that you have seen us indeed, and that we came this way when you were sowing your wheat'. Leaving the men to ponder over this cryptic message, the Family hurried on their way. Almost before they were out of sight, a miracle happened, and 'the new-sown grain sprang up high and immediately ripened to harvest', so that the peasants sent men back to their village to limber up the carts 'ready to bring home in the evening ripe sheaves from the wheat which they had sown that very morning'. A few moments later, Herod's soldiers appeared on the scene and asked the expected question. They were given the truthful answer that such a group had indeed passed that way, but at seed time; which convinced these simple fellows, who saw the ripened harvest before

overleaf
55 On the road to Egypt—Joseph has his carpenter's tools and the ox goes with them. Painted glass panel in Temple Ewell Church, near Dover.

opposite
56 The mountain is divided: the escape of Elizabeth and the infant St John. Mosaic in the Kariye Camii, Istanbul, fourteenth century.

57 The miracle of the wheatfield, and the interrogation of the peasants by Herod's troops. Detail of the Rest on the Flight, by an Antwerp master, 1519.

their eyes, that they were on a fool's errand. It seemed useless for them to search any longer in that quarter, so they gave up the chase and turned back, and the family was saved by an apt and convenient miracle.

In its dexterity, in its alliance of truth with cunning, this story is unlike any of the other tales which stud the lives of the Holy Family in their journeys and in their stay in Egypt. Had it been known to any of the apocryphal writers, they would have undoubtedly have set it down; but it appears in no apocryphal writing. Its origins are altogether unknown: yet early in the fourteenth century it suddenly appeared full-blown in the works of several geographically scattered but more or less contemporary writers. There is a theory which at least bears examination, that it is an adaptation of a northern fertility myth, perhaps from the remoter Baltic provinces in which Christianity was only then taking root under the untender hands of the Teutonic Knights. But whatever its source, it was immensely popular throughout Europe and in most pictures of the Flight, and in many of those of the 'Rest on the Flight', one can see, somewhere in the background, the scene of Herod's troops—generally mounted men—who are questioning or threatening the reapers of the miraculous harvest. All mediaeval people would have understood the message of these little vignettes, which reminded men of the neat story of the power and wit of Mary, who by 'diddling' without an untruth the men at arms of wicked old Herod had saved the lives of that little group on which, in the end, every man's hope of salvation lay. A very ancient English song, 'The Carnal' (the crow) 'and the Crane', in which the leading role is given to Jesus, sets out the tale in this way:

> Then Jesus, ah! and Joseph,
> And Mary that was unknown,
> They travelled by a husbandman
> Just when his seed was sown.

> 'God speed thee, man!' said Jesus,
> 'Go fetch thy ox and wain
> And carry home the corn again
> Which thou this day hast sown. . . .

> If any should come this way
> And enquire for me alow,
> Tell them that Jesus passèd,
> As thou thy seed did sow.'

> After that there came King Herod
> With his train so furiously,
> Enquiring of the husbandsman
> Whether Jesus passèd by.

> 'Why the truth it must be spoken
> And the truth it must be known,
> For Jesus passèd this way
> When my seed was sown.

> But now I have it reapen
> And some laid on my wain,
> Ready to fetch and carry
> Into my barn again'.

'Turn back', said the captain,
'Your labour and mine's in vain
It's full three quarters of a year
Since he his seed has sown'.

So Herod was deceivèd
By the work of God's own hand.
And further they proceeded
Into the Holy Land.

So the family escaped from Herod's wrath, and as far as we know they crossed the southern border of Judea without further alarms and could allow themselves, gratefully, to rest in their flight.

Soon, they would be followed on the road by other fugitives, for back in Bethlehem a second 'Flight' was preparing; and in Jerusalem, a murder. Jesus, Herod's first intended victim, had escaped him. But now that the wise men, the predictors of the future, had slipped from his grasp, how could he be sure that this Jesus had really been the predestined one he so much feared? News had come to him of a child John, whose birth had been attended by disquieting portents and who was now in Bethlehem, the suspect city, with his mother Elizabeth. This he thought, could perhaps be he whose existence would threaten his throne, and his son's succession. He fell into the same confusion between the two children as his grandson Herod Antipas was to know, years later, when both the children were grown men and mighty teachers in the land of Israel: after this Antipas, for what seemed to be a dancer's whim, had beheaded this John who had become the Baptist, he heard the certain news of one in Israel who performed miracles and cast out devils and healed the sick. This, surprisingly enough in the ruler of the territory in which Jesus had spent much of his ministry and where he had done these same things, could for him, for Antipas, be only one man. Seized with superstitious dread he cried out *It is John, whom I beheaded: he is risen from the dead . . . mighty works do show forth themselves in him*. What were these mighty works which he had performed, we do not know. John's followers—and they were many—stood a little apart from those of Jesus, and were probably of a different but allied persuasion. None of their writings have survived, or have been allowed to survive; and it is perhaps for this reason that this *man sent from God* of whom the Jews asked *art thou Elias?* has not attained a higher place in the Christian pantheon.

Herod the Great, in his time, could certainly take no chances with this child, this John, who might be he whom the wise men had sought; and he sent his troops to Bethlehem to search for him particularly by name, and to kill him. Elizabeth heard of this just in time, and fled to the hills with Herod's men in hot pursuit: she 'looked for somewhere to hide him; and there was no place of concealment. And Elizabeth groaned, and said in a loud voice, Mount of God, receive a mother with

56 her child. And suddenly the mountain was divided and received her'. The 'angel of the Lord' was with them, and the mountain closed again behind them, leaving the soldiery baffled and helpless. Elizabeth continued her flight, but the troops could only report back to Herod that mother and son had disappeared, swallowed up by the ground in extraordinary and certainly magical circumstances.

Herod was enraged when he heard of their escape, which by its nature confirmed all his worst fears. In this year, John's father Zacharias — a little of whose history we find in the first chapter of Luke — was High Priest of the Temple of Jerusalem. Herod viewed him with the deepest suspicion. A high priest was certainly versed in sorcery and occult practices, and it was surely he who had caused his wife and his son John to vanish. Zacharias himself, busy with his great duties in the Temple, did not yet seem to have known what had happened in Bethlehem, but Herod, in the words of the Protevangelium, sent his servants to him saying:

> Where hast thou hidden thy son? And he answered and said unto them, I am the minister of God and am busied with the Temple of the Lord. I do not know where my son is. And the servant went away, and reported to Herod all these things, and Herod was angry, and said, His son is going to be King of Israel. And he sent to him again, saying, Tell the truth, where is thy son? For thou knowest that thy blood is under my hand. And Zacharias said, I am a witness to God, if thou dost shed my blood; for the Lord will receive my spirit, for thou sheddest innocent blood in the porch of the Lord's Temple. And about

58 daybreak, Zacharias was slain.

The deed was done in secret in the Sanctuary, where the High Priest alone was allowed to go. When, early in the morning, the officiating priests of the day arrived at their stations in the body of the Temple and waited there for their orders, wondering uneasily why Zacharias had not come out to greet them, a 'great voice' cried out:

> Zacharias is murdered. His blood shall not be wiped out till the avenger cometh . . . and the wainscotings of the Temple shrieked out, and the curtains were split from top to bottom.

58 The murder of Zacharias in the Holy of Holies in the Temple of Jerusalem. After a mural from Gračanica Monastery, Yugoslavia, *c.* 1320.

One of the priests ventured into the Sanctuary. The body of Zacharias was not there, and was never to be found. But before the High Altar of the Holy of Holies his blood was upon the ground, hard 'like stone' and never to be cleansed away.

Zacharias's blood became a notable relic. The lady whom we call the 'Bordeaux Pilgrim', who visited Jerusalem in the year 333, was the first of the hundreds who have written accounts of their travels in the Holy Land; and she was duly shown the bloodstains '. . . in this building where stood the Temple which Solomon built . . . There are also to be seen the marks of the nails in the shoes of the soldiers who slew him, throughout the whole enclosure, so plain that you would think that they were impressed with wax'. Her trip was not a comfortable one, for in her day the reception of pilgrims had not yet been put on a proper basis by the local inhabitants; and it was not to be so until some sixty years later, when a suitable tourist organisation was created for the benefit of the elegant women who crowded to Bethlehem to sit at the feet of St Jerome and who, with their trains of servants, would invariably make a round of the Holy Places. Antoninus Martyr, for instance, a gay and perceptive pilgrim who was there in the year 570, remarks that a steep entry charge was made for a view of Zacharias's blood, which was evidently still a popular attraction; and he also tells us that in his day Christ's tomb was plated with silver and gold and so gaudily decorated that 'it had the appearance of a winning post on a race-course'. In the succeeding centuries, with the convenient re-discovery of the many instruments of the Passion and the identification of the sites connected with it and with every Christian scene, memorials of a more strictly Jewish kind tended to be pushed into the background in the hurly-burly of the conducted pilgrimages of mediaeval times, which sometimes covered the Holy Land in as little as eleven days of mule-back travelling; but 'Zacharias's blood', even in the fifteenth century, was still visited by more leisured pilgrims.

Elizabeth and her son, for their part, eventually reached Egypt in their turn, and seem to have wandered there for some time. The 'Life of John according to Serapion' has it that after five years Elizabeth died on a mountainside in the wilderness of 'Ain Kārim, leaving John an orphan of 'only seven years and six months old'; from which we can take as some additional evidence that Jesus himself had reached the age of seven at this stage of his life in Egypt, though Serapion, with in-different history, confuses us by his statement that 'Herod also died on the same day as the blessed Elizabeth'. The young John did not know how to shroud and bury his mother, but Jesus himself, 'because she was his mother's kinswoman came down from the clouds to help him' and brought with him the faithful Salome, who washed the body. The archangels Michael and Gabriel descended from Heaven to dig the grave, and the souls of her husband Zacharias, and of old Simeon of the Temple, sang her threnody. Mary was there too, and her tender heart urged her to take the orphan into her charge, but Jesus told her that this was not God's will, and that he should remain in the wilderness until 'the day of his showing unto Israel'. But the child remained with them until the days of mourning were over, and a passage in this curious work tells us that Mary and Jesus 'taught him how to live in the desert', a desert for him which was to be innocent of wild beasts and filled with angels and prophets; where he may early have acquired a taste for locusts and wild honey.

8 The journey to the Nile

The apocryphal writers were indifferent geographers and none of them tell us which road the Family took in their journey to the Delta of the Nile. It was at least recorded as a 'wilderness' march, a 'desert way'; and at one stage when Mary complained that 'this heat broils us'—which is a curious saying to record in a journey which we ought to think of as having taken place in January—Joseph considered whether he should 'hold our course by the sea, that we may rest in the towns on the coast'. But they did not do so, for this seemed an unsafe route to take while they were still in Herod's lands, and we can reasonably assume that instead of taking the well-trodden route through Askalon and the fertile coastal plain they struck directly southwards, flanking the mountains of Judea, and reached the ill-defined border somewhere in the country beyond Beersheba. On this route, through sparsely inhabited territory, they would have been less likely to meet with military patrols, and less exposed to prying eyes. It would indeed have taken them through the bad lands of Sinai, the territory of the Edomites whom the Essenes, in their 'War Rule', a document almost exactly contemporary with the flight, had listed as the first of the unbelievers to be destroyed in the Last Days; but this may have been a specifically Essene view, for of all the adventures and dangers which they were to experience, none came from the hostility of those nomads through whose grounds they passed.

The Sinai of the twentieth century is a pitiless desert which the ill-equipped little party would have had the greatest difficulty in crossing, but in Joseph's and Mary's time, if we are to judge by the number of hermits who were to inhabit it in the early Christian centuries, it was less horrid than it is today. These hermits, or anchorites, with the exception of the truly saintly and ascetic Desert Fathers of Egypt, were seldom as uncomfortable in their lives as we often imagine them to have been. Their temporary or permanent retreats to the 'desert' did not necessarily mean more, in mediaeval parlance, than that they left town and lived as shepherds and charcoal burners did, 'without the pale', on uncultivated land, or in the forest, where they or a convenient acolyte would build themselves a hut not less comfortable than that in which most people lived; or they might instal themselves in a cave in what might appear to us, with our inheritance of the nineteenth-century views of the intrinsic beauties of nature, to be an agreeable hillside. St Jerome, in his famous retreat to the 'desert', had a well-stocked library, a prolific vegetable and herb garden, a purling stream, and plenty of visitors; and even the pillar saints such as Simeon Stylites generally did rather well from the offerings which they hauled up from their followers below, or which were handed to them from the top of convenient ladders.

There must, then, have been at least a sprinkling of suitable oases and some sort of grazing land in the Sinai of those days, and in travelling across it the Holy Family only once, as far as we know, suffered any real lack of food and drink. The story of the occasion is a famous one. The little group were plodding their way southward at a donkey's pace, and provisions had been short for some time. Joseph, as Pseudo-Matthew tells us, was anxious, for water was 'failing in their bottles', food was short, and Mary was 'wearied by the too great heat of the sun in the desert'. There was that lack of shade which every traveller in arid places knows, and when they came to a palm tree Mary gratefully sat down and rested for a while beneath it. Looking upwards, she saw ropes of ripe dates in the fronds above her, and called to Joseph to get her some of this fine fruit; but the clusters were far beyond his reach and he had no means of scaling the trunk. Mary, weakened by the journey, was chagrined and querulous, and a wearied Joseph spoke sharply to her; but in this moment of difficulty and discord the child Jesus brought about the first of all his miracles. He spoke out loud and clear and called on the palm tree to yield up its harvest to his mother: 'And straightway at this word the palm bowed down its top to the feet of the blessed Mary, and they gathered from it fruit by which all were re-freshed. And when they had gathered all its fruit, it remained bowed down, waiting to rise again at the command of him at whose word it had bowed down.'

The miracle of Mary with the wheat, and the palm tree story, this earliest manifestation of the powers of her son, became more popular in the West than any other of the events which marked the flight to Egypt. In artifacts of every kind from carved stone to stained glass to tapestries and hangings and a multitude of paintings, we see this palm tree paying its useful homage to Mary. Sometimes the whole trunk curves from the root, often with the help of angels who, even though they were held to be weightless beings, bear down gallantly upon it; and sometimes, particularly in the Iberian tradition, it is the fronds and the fruit which seem to reach down to offer themselves. The artist almost always had a reasonably clear idea of what the fronds looked like, for they were much used in Levantine countries for wadding bales of merchandise which would have found their way to every European market place, and he generally knew that the trunk of the tree had some sort of a scaly appearance; but it was rare that he had actually seen a tree or its fruit, so that he had difficulty in imagining what a stick of dates looked like. The fruit sometimes took on a quite peculiar aspect, and was shown in the manner of pine kernels, or perhaps like plums; but if one knows the story the intention is clear.

67   The palm tree itself, suffering more than one metamorphosis, took on local colour. Sometimes in Germany and in the northern countries of the great pine forests, it becomes a pine or fir tree, changing completely its original shape and outline. It was sometimes seen in France as an orange tree; and it crops up in another guise in the 'Golden Legend' of Jacobus Voraginus: 'Cassiodorus saith in the history Tripartite, in Hermopolis of Thebaid there was a tree called Persidis which is medicinal for all sickness, for if a leaf or rind of that tree is bound to the neck of a sick person, it healeth it anon, and as the Blessed Virgin Mary fled with her son, the tree bowed down and worshipped Jesu Christ'. The 'tree called Persidis' is the peach tree, *Persicum malum,* the Persian apple; and 'Hermopolis of Thebaid'—of Egypt—we shall come upon a little later in the journey. In England—and elsewhere—the palm tree, or at least its story, was turned into the cherry tree, whose fruit, when it was first introduced into Europe from Asia Minor in the middle ages, was thought to have a delicacy and a fragrance beyond comprehension; which in turn, and in a typical mediaeval thought-process, led through mystical symbolism to it becoming one of the emblems of Jesus. From the English 'Cherry Tree' tradition comes the old song which bears that name, and which changes all things about: the miracle of the bending tree happens before the birth of Jesus, who speaks up from his mother's womb; the desert becomes a Kentish orchard; and we hear again the ancient echoes of Joseph's distrust of Mary's strange tale of the origins of her pregnancy:

> Joseph was an old man,
>   And an old man was he,
> When he wedded Mary
>   In the land of Galilee . . .
>
> Joseph and Mary walked
>   Through an orchard green,
> There were berries and cherries
>   As thick as might be seen.

O then bespoke Mary
   So meek and so mild
'Pluck me one cherry, Joseph,
   For I am with child'.

O then bespoke Joseph,
   With words most unkind
'Let him pluck the cherry,
   That brought thee with child'.

O then bespoke the babe
   Within his mother's womb —
'Bow down then the tallest tree
   For my mother to have some'.

Then bowed down the highest tree,
   Unto his mother's hand,
Then she cried, 'See, Joseph,
   I have cherries at command'.

O then bespake Joseph —
   'I have done Mary wrong;
But cheer up my dearest,
   And be not cast down' . . .

Then Mary plucked a cherry,
   As red as the blood;
Then Mary went home,
   With her heavy load . . .

In the original desert and palm tree setting of the apocryphals, Jesus completes the family's present blessings by causing a hidden spring which had been concealed beneath the roots of the palm to well up to the surface as 'a most pure fount of water, very cool and exceedingly clear', so that not only the family but 'all the beasts and cattle were satisfied': an echo, in Pseudo-Matthew, of those flocks and herds which some supposed that they — and necessarily their herdsmen, whose presence would have quite changed the picture — had driven before them from Judea.

In the story the tree had remained bent down, waiting a further command: 'Jesus, turning to the palm tree, said "this privilege I grant you that one of your branches shall be taken by my angels and planted in the Paradise of my father. And this blessing I will confer on you, that of all who have conquered in a contest it may be said that they have attained the palm of victory. And as he said these things, behold, an

59 From the fronds of the miraculous palm, the angel plucks a 'Palm of Victory'. Detail from the Rest on the Flight by Joachim Patenier, early sixteenth century.

angel of the Lord appeared, standing above the palm tree; and taking away one of its branches he flew to heaven having the branch in his hand.' The 'Palm of Victory', together with the bay and the laurel, was known as a symbol of victory in the ancient world, and Cicero writes of it more than once; but it was through this story that the term came to the west, and this is the origin of the 'palms of victory' of which we still speak today, and to which the continental nations of Europe are still excessively partial.

Rested and refreshed, the little group went on their way, and in the evening of the next day, 'when they had come to a certain cave and wished to rest in it, the blessed Mary came down from the beast [the donkey] and sat and held the child Jesus in her lap . . . and suddenly there came out of the cave many dragons. . . . Then Jesus, descending from his mother's lap, stood on his feet before the dragons, and they adored Jesus and then departed from them'. In almost every apocryphal book concerned with his childhood Jesus had this calming power, not only over sinister and magical beasts such as dragons, but over wild animals of every kind. 'Lions and leopards', for example, 'adored him, and kept company with them in the desert; whithersoever Mary and Joseph went, they went before them, showing the way and bowing their heads; and showing subjection by wagging their tails, they adored him with great reverence'. Jesus, it was said, walked fearlessly into a cavern where there was a lioness and her whelps, which fawned at his feet, and there is even a northern gloss to this conception in a tale of Jesus walking among wolves. These pious 'power-and-reverence' stories, which were given prominence largely to astonish the mediaeval masses, and to demonstrate the power of the child over all creation, may yet have a core of truth within them; and they may be based on

60 'Dragons' menace the Family on their journey, but Jesus pacifies them with a gesture. From a fourteenth-century Italian manuscript.

an older tradition of the family in their flight in danger from wild beasts, and of their escape from them: a story which we should expect, and do not find.

By now, the journey from Bethlehem had already been long, and at about this stage of it we can conveniently place that 'Rest on the Flight to Egypt', which was in mediaeval times, and later, so popular a conception that pictures of it can be found in every considerable picture gallery of the world. For this more or less prolonged halt on the way to Egypt, there are traces of Levantine tradition, but no proper apocryphal justification. It is possible that the original idea of this 'Resting time' may have been invented by the Crusaders, and it was certainly they who popularised it throughout Europe. Whatever had been their original ideas of conquest and *Lebensraum* in the East, they were keenly aware that in Palestine—and in Egypt too—they were on holy ground. Many of them had actually been in Egypt, and even reached the Nile, either on ill-starred campaigns or, if they were great barons with their suites, for whom it was often quite easy to arrange safe-conducts which carried them deep into Muslim country, they travelled as pilgrims or tourists; making, no doubt, a suitable reconnaissance on their way. The Holy Family was much in their thoughts, and as they travelled over the road which they had taken in past times, they understood how long and arduous their journey had been; and it was evident to them that that awkward and rather helpless little party of an elderly man, accompanied by a young girl and her baby, and perhaps by Salome, must have made at least one halt of a day or two on the way. The idea of the 'Rest' had come to stay.

In the late mediaeval centuries the theme of the Rest as an integral part of the Flight—but which required a far more complex picture than those of the Flight itself—became a grateful one to painters. They added other incidents, which belong to quite other stages of the journey to Egypt, to the pictures of the Flight, and soon we find that springs gush up, wheat fields have grown, trees bend down with luscious fruit and angels descend with gifts and provisions of every kind. On a more terrestrial plane, Mary—or even angels—attend to practical matters such as the washing of the family's linen, while Joseph wanders off to the mill, and the donkey, at grass but unhobbled, gets a needed rest. Visitors come to call on them, such as the young John the Baptist, or St Anne, appearing out of nowhere, or Trypho the friendly robber. And there is the little-known story of the gypsy woman who startled Mary by the suddenness with which she appeared before her. She asks to tell her child's fortune and to read his future and, with Mary's permission, she proceeds to do so with a startling accuracy which leads her even to the scene of the Resurrection itself. When

61 The Rest on the Flight, and the appearance of the gipsy. By Paris Bordone, sixteenth century.

Mary offers to cross her palm with silver for her pains, she declines with politeness and modesty and asks instead that, if her prophecies prove true, she should be granted free passage at the last to the gates of Heaven. An Italian canzonetta, probably of the sixteenth century, tells the story in detail, but we know of no earlier sources, and the song itself has been forgotten. Gypsies did not appear in Italy until the fifteenth century and one would imagine that it would have taken some generations for them to take their place in popular folklore. Representations of the scene are in any case exceedingly rare—or perhaps unrecognised— for the picture by Paris Bordone, which was first identified by the great Mrs. A. B. Jameson in the forties of the last century when it was hanging as a Giorgione in the long gallery of the Shrewsbury house of Alton Towers, is now in the fine arts museum at Strasbourg, and still bears the label 'The Rest on the Flight with the Virgin and St Anne'.

The Rest had many attractions for painters of later times which the Flight itself could not offer. The hardships and privations which the family had suffered on the journey itself were in one sense self-inflicted for it was clear to everyone that Jesus, to whom all things were possible, could have alleviated them with a gesture. In pictures of the Flight, therefore, it was normal to indicate, in one way or another, the pilgrim-like simplicity of the Holy Family and the ardours of the journey to which these great ones of the earth had deliberately, as it were, exposed themselves. Moreover the simple composition of the donkey and the little family party moving from left to right across the panel—for movement from right to left generally meant a 'Return' from Egypt to Nazareth—became in time hackneyed and repetitive. So it seemed to men even before the Renaissance had begun, and the Holy Family in this simple guise was little seen from the late fourteenth century until that much later time when other generations of painters could offer themselves all the pleasures of a bosky and elegant landscape as the setting for this journey. But the Rest was quite a different matter. Local treatment of sacred subjects had of course always been normal, and every painter moved the setting from an unimaginable Sinai to his own country and his own landscape. And in this case, for these mediaeval and early Renaissance painters whose freedom of composition was still restricted by tradition and their patron's requirements, a certain liberty in the treatment of the scene can be observed from a relatively early date. The Rest had been a time of repose, of relaxation, which in itself seems to have invited a measure of freedom in the grouping of the essential figures and to have given an opportunity to introduce extraneous characters and events in a bucolic setting. This did not suit the painters of Byzantium with their rigid traditionalism. But in the West, from the middle of the sixteenth century, this 'Rest on the Flight to Egypt' began to turn into a picnic, or a *fête champêtre*. The benefit is ours.

The Holy Family moved on refreshed, but before they were to reach Egypt they were to experience a whole series of happenings. Some are of little interest, some are re-enacted during the years of exile, and we will restrict ourselves to the story of 'The Robber Trypho and his Belt'. The tale is best given in the Arabic Gospel of the Infancy, though this calls Trypho 'Titus': '. . . as they went, they saw two robbers, lying [on watch] in the way, and with them a multitude of robbers, their companions, who were asleep. Titus said to Dumachus, I beg of you to let these persons depart freely, and unobserved by our companions who are sleeping. But when Dumachus refused, he yet urged him not to open his mouth or speak, and held out to him as a pledge the belt with which he was girded and which contained within it thirty

opposite
62 Mary before the Palm Tree, an exquisite miracle. From the left wing reverse panel of a Flemish triptych depicting the Miracles of Christ, oil on wood, fifteenth century.

overleaf
63 The Rest on the Flight to Egypt. Studio of Patenier, early sixteenth century.

64 The arrival at Hermopolis, with a reminder of the palm tree; and the fall of the idol (middle ground on the right). Some of Joseph's tools lie on the ground. School of Cologne, *c.* 1500.

drachmas, which he offered to him for his silence. And when the lady Mary saw that the robber showed kindness to them, she said The Lord God shall sustain thee with his right hand, and shall give thee remission of your sins . . . and they passed on unharmed'.

These two, Trypho and Dumachus, were the good and the bad thieves who many years later were roped to their crosses—'hung on the tree'—and died with Jesus at Golgotha, casting in his teeth, in Matthew and Mark, his inability to save them. It is Luke who establishes a difference between them, and has Jesus say to the good thief, *Today shalt thou be with me in paradise;* and in mediaeval pictures, when a distinction is made—and it usually is—between the two robbers hanging in their bonds, Trypho is shown on the left hand of Jesus, though of course this is the right hand (which is what counted in mediaeval times) of the spectator, and his eyes will be raised to his promised Heaven, while Dumachus looks downward to the Hell in

65 The Family attacked by Robbers. From the Holkham Bible Picture Book, an English manuscript of the second quarter of the fourteenth century.

the bowels of the earth below him which he knows will be his lot. The thirty shekels which had been in Trypho's belt, and which he had given to Dumachus on that day in the desert long before to buy the escape of the Holy Family from his fellow thieves, became thirty pieces of silver, a 'thirty pieces of silver' which had an astonishing and complex history which is set out in a later version of Saloman of Bassovah's 'Book of the Bee': they had been struck in old time by Terah, who 'took Abram his son, and Lot . . . and went forth with them from Ur of the Chaldees to go into the land of Canaan'. Abraham inherited them, as did his son Isaac and — to telescope their history — they came into David's hands, who gave them to Solomon who put them round the door of the altar of the Temple. Nebuchadnezzar took them to Babylon as spoils of war; and eventually they came into the hands of the Magi, who used them on their journey to Bethlehem to buy from shepherds in Edessa the garment without a seam which the shepherds had received from an angel; and they fell into the hands of a robber who used them to save Joseph — here is our Trypho and Dumachus — and were recovered by the men of King Abgar of Edessa who sent them to Jesus, hoping that he would visit him; but Jesus gave them to the Treasury of the Temple, and they were the thirty pieces of silver which the priests gave to Judas Iscariot for his betrayal of his Lord. Judas repented of his bitter deed and cast them down on the floor of the Sanctuary *and departed, and went and hanged himself. And the chief priests took the silver*

66 A royal reception at the Egyptian border.

pieces . . . and they took counsel, and bought with them the potter's field, to bury strangers in. And from the stranger's ground, the potter's field, we know no more of them.

To return to our travellers: Joseph led his charges over the last of Sinai to the confines of Egypt, where according to a Byzantine tradition they were received with signal honours at the border fortress which lay on their way. Frescoes show them, often accompanied by a young man —in the Byzantine history, one of Joseph's sons—and with one or several personages coming through the gates to salute them, showing, with their knees a little bent as they advance, and with their hands sometimes hidden in the folds of their garment, the signs of respect due to princes.

The Holy Family moved on again on that last lap of their journey which was to take them to the Delta of the Nile. As they approached that fertile land, the first town which they came to was usually called Hermopolis, of which there were three in Egypt at the time; or, better, the town of Sotinen in the province of Hermopolis. This was a great walled city, and according to the 'Arabic' Gospel, it had in its centre a great idol with a resounding voice; and every word it said was reported to all the inhabitants of Egypt and of all its borders. But at the approach of Jesus, it crashed to the ground in irretrievable ruin, just as the idols of the Ka'aba were to tumble from their pedestals at the approach of Muhammed. Pseudo-Matthew has it that in the town of Sotinen there were no less than three hundred and sixty-five idols, each with its day of worship in the year, and that they all fell together in a moment of time. Aphrodisius the high priest heard the thunderous noise of their destruction and ran to the temple—though the 'Arabic' version has it that Aphrodisius was the king of that province who came with all his army—and seeing this chaos sought for the cause of the fall of his Gods. Joseph and Mary, with Jesus, were still outside the city walls and when at last he came upon them he recognised immediately their special quality, and hastened to prostrate himself before this new and greater power which had come to supplant the ancient deities of Egypt.

Aphrodisius the king prostrated himself likewise, but he was a prudent man, and reflected that if he did not put himself at once and unreservedly at the service of this new deity who was present in the flesh before him, he and his men might 'incur the peril of his indignation, and we may all come to destruction as befell Pharaoh, king of the Egyptians; who not believing such miracles, was drowned with all his army in the sea'. Western tradition did not know of the incident of the royal reception at the marcher castle, so that for the West this man was the first of all the pagans of the world who had the honour of being converted by Jesus himself to the new faith and the new law, and this

66

64

64

67 Journeying into Egypt, with the 'palm tree' and the ox. After Dürer's *Life of Mary*, from the Nonnberg High Altar, Salzburg, 1515.

first proselyte to the Christian religion occupied for many centuries a special place in the Christian hierarchy. It was believed that he established the faith of Jesus in all Egypt, and that after some years of ministry he crossed the sea to Gaul, where he converted multitudes; and that he ended his life as the first bishop and eventually the patron saint of Béziers, in the Aude, near the eastern Pyrénées. And this antique king of Hermopolis, as St Aphrodise, is still remembered by many in that city of wine, though sometimes with ribaldry because of his name.

9 Life in Egypt

Many of the apocryphal books tell us something of the life of the Holy Family in Egypt. The origin of these works, as far as we can tell, lie in widely scattered areas of the eastern Mediterranean; and as the canon is entirely silent on the matter they are our only source books for the history of the family at this particular period of their lives. Unfortunately, their contents differ considerably from one work to another, and each is marked with such imprecision in time and place and order that they can give but a limited satisfaction to an enquiring mind. Events which they record are sometimes peculiar to a single text, or group of texts having a similar origin, and may reflect local traditions which had perhaps been transferred from elsewhere and attributed to the childhood of Jesus. In some cases a record of the same or similar events appears in several separate works, each of which presents it in a manner which may have been suitable to the customs or theological tendencies of a particular area. Some of the stories which they tell clearly owe their origin to the oriental folklore and superstition which form the basis for story cycles such as the Arabian Nights, and which here are bent to Christian and pious ends.

In considering these reservations, which affect a greater or lesser degree all the apocryphal works which deal with the life of the family in exile, we have to remember that from the earliest days of Christianity no one in authority, and no organisation with a continuous existence, had any interest in maintaining the integrity of the early apocryphal texts. The contrary, indeed, was the case, for all of them were officially anathematised by the Christian Establishment, and the semi-clandestine conditions under which they continued to exist allowed local or regional schools of thought, sometimes heretical, but more often exaggeratedly pietistic and Marial, to bend them as they wished: and they have never, until the most recent times, had the benefit of solid recension or exegesis.

These reservations, stated with extreme brevity, are not particularly encouraging to the general reader, and they are daunting to the few, the very few exact scholars who have scrutinised the available material. Yet our abiding wonder should be that, given their earlier conditions of existence, so many of the texts survived at all, and survived in a form and with a content which often does approximate to such original elements as we know and sometimes, in the few cases in which we can summon independent evidence, can match it fairly closely. Important non-Christian writings give us many cross-checks; and we hear echoes of the apocryphal childhood in ancient traditions persistently maintained. We are not dealing here with such material as the recently discovered nilotic Gospel of Thomas, with its noble logions, or ancient fragments such as the Oxyrhynchus papyrus with

68 The First Steps of Jesus: walking aids of this kind were not uncommon particularly in Eastern Europe: Mary is spinning the True Purple. By the 'Master of the Choirs of Jesus', fifteenth century.

its variations to the teachings of Jesus, although these are themselves in the strict sense of the term 'apocryphal' works. But in our own field, of the Holy Family and the childhood of Jesus, we do possess, for example, in the Protevangelium of James, a second-century work as old, or almost as old, as the Gospels, for which we have a complete manuscript of the third century already showing evident traces of emendation, yet which is older than almost any of the New Testament manuscripts which have survived; and the Gospel of Thomas is only a little less ancient. They cannot but be treated with respect; and if our approach to other infancy writings should be more cautious, we cannot deny all credence to some of their passages and to some of their tales, which lie at the heart of the very beginnings of the Christian story.

Had the Protevangelium continued its history beyond the departure of the Wise Men and the killing of the Innocents it would have been very much to our purpose, for it might have given us a more authoritative solution to our first problem concerning the life of the Holy Family in Egypt: where, in fact, did they live? The apocryphals are miserly in geographic detail, but it does appear from them that they spent most of their years of exile in one of the big villages — or small towns — of the Delta of the Nile, where they became well-known and where Joseph found work, perhaps of a spasmodic kind, as a carpenter. The source books give us the names of various places, or of none; but we shall opt without hesitation for the township which is most solidly anchored in tradition: Materea, a few miles north of the present centre of Cairo, 'el-Matariyeh', a place of many ancient marvels, and of one very recent one. Materea was the end of their journey. And the inhabitants of the town, of whatever persuasion, and until quite recent times, have found solid advantage in perpetuating and promoting this early association with the life of Jesus and Mary.

Since very early Christian times — and almost certainly before — a tree in Materea has been held to be particularly sacred. We can trace its history through almost two thousand years, watch it change through the centuries in bewildering succession from palm to sycamore to fig, and to sycamore again, and observe the stories which accrete about it. We think of the tree itself, and wonder at the changes. But it was the spot which was sacred, as a sacred grove might be, and the Christian West which multiplied the prepuce of the infancy or the nails of the Passion of its protagonist has never been in a position to criticise these metamorphoses. Under the shade of this great tree, it was said, the Holy Family had rested at last at the end of their journey; which made it easy, in later times, to modify this concept into the 'Rest on the

69 Jesus and his companions playing at marbles and spinning tops; on the right they clash pottery vessels together; Jesus' pot is indestructible. Detail from fourteenth-century panel.

Flight' itself and to assert that this tree was the palm which had bowed down before them. In the first centuries of our era, when this Christian tradition was still fresh, it was in fact a palm, and when the theologian Sozomen came that way in about the year 425 he was shown this tree which, he said, 'had a particularly sacred character to all the inhabitants of Egypt': a country which was at the time, of course, fanatically, if sometimes heretically, Christian. About two centuries later a chapel in honour of the Virgin was built at the spot and the sacred tree became, in the first of its variants, a sycamore under which the family had halted — in another throwback to the Flight — when their bottles and skins were empty. Leaving Jesus under the tree, Mary had gone in search of water and when she returned she found that the child, drumming with his

opposite
70 The family in Joseph's workshop — notice Mary's workbasket, Jesus' toys, and the cockroaches. From a Spanish manuscript, fifteenth century.

overleaf
71 Jesus makes sparrows from clay and instils life into them. Ceiling painting in St Martin's Church, Zillis, Switzerland, twelfth century.

heels on the ground, had caused a limpid spring to gush forth with such force and volume that all their needs were satisfied; and in later days the Muslims were able to canalise these waters into a public bath so vast that three hundred people could enter it at once.

The Muslims themselves believed that Mary and Jesus had lived in the town. They revered the tree beneath which their third prophet and his mother had first rested, and under their tolerant rule many Christian pilgrims visited this sycamore. Crusaders who came to Egypt for conquest or on pilgrimages reported the famous tree to be of gigantic size, and when Almaric the Prince-Archbishop of Narbonne led his force of Franks and Greeks to the Delta in an abortive campaign, his tent was pitched for the night beneath its branches on a November evening in 1168. By the fourteenth and fifteenth centuries Materea had become an elegant suburb of New Cairo, the greatest city of the world, but according to traveller's accounts its ancient sycamore had been replaced by an immense fig tree, in the hollow of whose trunk Jesus and Mary, in a curious throwback to an earlier time and place, were said to have hidden from Herod's men; and at the foot of this tree, visitors were told, the child had caused water to spring in a time of drought. Roberto da Sanseverino, nephew of Duke Francesco Sforza of Milan, saw the tree in 1458 and walked in the magnificent garden of balsam trees which then surrounded it. The bushes, to which there are oblique references from early times, were then the jealously guarded property of the Sultan of Egypt, who extracted and sold their precious oil, and the tradition of the time had it that the original plants had been given to King Solomon by the Queen of Sheba and that at a later day they had been transplanted to Materea and set about this hallowed fig tree. The author of the Arabic Gospel knew something of this story, though his information was certainly at no better than third or fourth hand. There had come to his ears one of those jumbled tales which, made up of disparate elements distorted by time and distance and hearsay, seem so often to confirm by their existence an underlying truth, and he wrote of 'a sycamore tree called Materea' where Jesus had summoned from the ground a fountain of water in which his mother had washed the family linen; and added that 'from the sweat which the Lord Jesus there let drop, balsam came forth in that region'.

74

overleaf
72 The 'Seven Wells' near Cairo, the pools which Jesus made when he played beside the river. From a French manuscript, fifteenth century.

opposite
73 Gathering in the miraculous harvest which Jesus had sown. From an English manuscript, c. 1300.

By da Sanseverino's time, the fig tree must have been in its declining years. The fig is a symbolic tree, but the sycamore, in a tradition far older than Mary, was the tree of Hathor the Mother, the Protectress, the tree of life on which the stars came to rest and from which they derived their eternal substance. And by the end of the next century, at the latest, the sycamore of Mary-Hathor was again present at the spot. Eighteenth-century travellers visited it; and the great tree which the Frankish Crusaders had seen long ago was matched by the gigantic specimen which was shown to their successors in Napoleon's army, spreading its great branches over the spot which was still pointed out to them as the place of the 'Rest', the halting place which marked the end of the flight; and here, they were told, was the town where the Holy Family had lived in exile. From the beginning of the British condominium in 1882, little more was heard of these ancient memories, the great tree seems to have been lost to view, and local tourist revenues would have shown a marked decline. Materea itself became enveloped in the suburb of Zeitun.

74 Mary in Materea washes the household linen in the spring beneath the sycamore. Beside it grows a tree of balsam. From the Holkham Bible Picture Book, second quarter of the fourteenth century.

But the tradition of the presence of the Holy Family lives on, and its remarkable tenacity showed itself in the happenings of as recent a date as the month of May 1968, when the miraculous appearance, on several successive nights, of the Virgin Mary on the dome of one of the churches of the town was solemnly verified by the Coptic Patriarch Kyrollos II, and thousands who had never heard of the apocryphal texts flocked to the spot, carrying her portrait and chanting hymns. On one night alone, no less than seven people died in the crush; and the swarming crowds of Copts and Catholics, Muslims and Orthodox, who still knew something of the connections of this place with Mary and Jesus in exile in their own country of Egypt, demonstrated perfectly the vividness with which folk memory, even today, can retain the substance of ancient and 'apocryphal' tales which have been handed down by word of mouth through almost two millennia. The event, which once would have stirred the Christian world, was hardly reported, save in a few paragraphs in *The Times* of London. Ecclesiastical hierarchies of every denomination may have wished to play down the 'miraculous' appearances of Mary before an impressionable people and they may even have been ignorant of the ancient associations of Materea with their own prime movers. But the apparent lack of interest with which they greeted not only the event itself, but the remarkable public reaction which it aroused, adds a coda to the embarrassment to which the Christian churches are prone when they are confronted by reminders of some of the homelier, but apocryphal— and remembered— stories of the earliest days of Christianity.

The conditions of the Holy Family's life in Egypt are difficult to establish. The Latin Gospel of Thomas tells us that in the early days of exile, when Jesus was three years old, they lived for a year in the house of a 'certain widow'. The arrangement does not seem to have been a good one, for the family was not an ordinary family, and it was therefore suspect; and when Jesus finally chose to bring a salted fish back to life and sweetness and to cause it to swim about in a basin, the widow took them for wizards or necromancers and with the hearty assent of her neighbours 'cast them out of her house with great haste'. It was not to be the only time that they would be driven from home. Moreover, persistent mediaeval tradition, for which we have no early source, had it that the family passed through a period of great poverty and a curiously jumbled story has it that Mary had to ask her neighbours for wool, which she could not pay for, in order to continue her work for the curtains of the Temple. At one stage they were in such distress that Mary had to beg their bread from door to door. This particular story was a popular one, and even preachers as genial as St Bernadino of Siena used it to content their hearers with their earthly condition.

Two hundred years before his time it had been particularly grateful to the first generation of Franciscans. The 'Three Companions', writing in 1246, recall that when one day at supper-time 'the man of God [St Francis] heard that the Blessed Virgin was so poor that she had naught to give her son to eat he sighed with heavy grief and leaving the table ate his bread on the bare ground'.

A happy solution to their troubles is hinted at in that 'Arabic Gospel of the Infancy', which has already provided us with some material, and from which we draw extensively in this chapter and the next. This work, which shows strong Marial tendencies, stems from a Syrian archetype, probably of the fifth century, which in its Arabic translation—the only source we have today—was known to Muhammed, and several of its stories, which may be late accretions, are to be found in the Koran. It tells us, for instance, that the Holy Family lived at one time in the guest house of 'a very famous prince' and that they were showered with gifts by his wife after they had cured her son of leprosy. The 'Arabic' Gospel is our only source for this tale, but more than a thousand years later and in quite another country we find a strange, a very distant echo of this story which may at least go back to a parallel source. In 1697, Andreas Galeazzi, the Cardinal Archbishop of Genoa, considering himself to be a suitable candidate for the succession to the old and ailing Pope Innocent XII, set out to secure exalted patronage. One of his moves was to order a set of paintings on 'biblical' subjects from Francisco Providone, who was then fashionable with the Italian clerical establishment, and to send them, in sumptuous frames and accompanied by an exquisitely bound manuscript in which their subject matter was explained, to King Louis XIV. Galeazzi did not become Pope and the king, or his advisers, thought so little of the paintings that for a century, until they were taken out and sold by the orders of the National Convention, they lay in the cellars of the palace of St Germain. One of these pictures, however, shows the Holy Family elegantly dressed in a luxurious setting. Joseph has his flowered rod in his hand, and encouraged by his parents an unsteady Jesus is taking, unaided, his 'First Steps'. The little group is, as the book of words tells us, in a residence of Prince Alsamandar Porlac, a great nobleman of Egypt, who took pity on the Holy Family in their time of need and installed them, apparently permanently, in one of his seven palaces. This strange tale, which comes to the surface in this unexpected quarter, is not known today from any other source. It has in its immediate favour the fact that the word 'Alsamandar' is a princely title, or a combination of princely titles, in a pre-Islamic Arabian tongue, and the virtual certainty that the archbishop, in his day and for this special purpose, did not invent the tale. Indeed, he treats it rather as one generally known; and it is probable that somewhere, still waiting to be discovered, is the text which will establish its origins.

Throughout the Egyptian years the child Jesus, we are told, was excessively active in performing miracles. The child's power over brute creation had not diminished since the journey to Egypt and there are at least three sources which tell us of his domination over serpents. In two of them his brother James—later the 'Just'—left the house to gather sticks for kindling; or herbs for pottage; or in the third, the Arabian version, and in a more telling image, he went to take the eggs from a partridge nest. A venomous serpent struck him, and other boys, his companions, carried him back to the house, where he was like to die. But Jesus, on whom he called in his distress, went to the nest and compelled the snake to return with him to the house, where it was made to suck out again the venom which it had discharged. 'Then the Lord Jesus cursed him, and he [the serpent] was instantly rent asunder; and the boy, being stroked by the hand of Jesus, became well again . . . and this was Simon the Canaanite of whom mention is made in the Gospel': and indeed, in Matthew, it is this Simon who is listed as the last of the Apostles, save Judas Iscariot.

On another and more famous occasion, Thomas tells us that 'Jesus, being five years old, was playing at the crossing of a stream, and he collected the running water into pools, and immediately made them pure; and by his word alone he commanded them. And having made soft clay, he fashioned out of it twelve sparrows'. But it was the Sabbath when he did this work, and other children who had been playing with him told their fathers that he had done that which it was unlawful to do on the day of rest; and the fathers told Joseph, who came down to the river to admonish his child. But Jesus, paying scant attention to his father's words, 'clapped his hands and cried to the sparrows and said to them, Go away: and the sparrows flew up and departed, making a noise'. This was one of the infancy stories which was known throughout Europe, and of which a curious variant occurs in Iceland. There, the birds which Jesus had created from clay were taken to be plovers, common in the island in the summer season. Their cry, a curious keening note, was held to resemble the Icelandic word for prayer; and so they were taken to be praying, and urging to prayer: holy birds, fitting birds for Jesus to fashion.

Healing miracles are many. Jesus' swaddling bands remained as potent as they had been in the case of Salome's withered hand and on one occasion, in exchange for one of them, Mary received a sumptuous

cloak from 'a woman called Mary, and the name of her son was Cleopas', though what these two—whom we shall meet later—were doing in Egypt at that time and in that relationship is not explained. Trachoma, an eye disorder, was probably as prevalent among the villagers of the Delta as it is today, but the water in which Jesus had washed had great power and was sovereign against it. Typically, a mother 'took a little of the water as lady Mary had said, and poured it on her son; and having done this, his pain ceased and when he had slept a little he afterwards awoke from sleep safe and sound'. Leprosy was cured by the same means, and in one throwback to the cave near Bethlehem, an Egyptian woman claimed to have passed by there by chance at the time of the birth and to have been cleansed of her disease by the water which had been used for bathing the new-born child. Naturally, she fervently recommends the cure; and when, for example, 'a part of the water which had been used [for bathing Jesus] was poured on to a girl who dwelt there and whose body was white with leprosy, she washed in it and was instantly cured'; and in the same way a leprous and rejected wife was cleansed of her disease and reunited with her husband. A bride struck deaf and dumb on her wedding day was restored to speech and hearing by holding Jesus in her arms. For the child simply to appear in the presence of the possessed was enough to drive out devils and evil spirits, and Satan himself in his primaeval role, coiled about the body of a woman in the guise of a serpent, fled in terror before him. Strangely enough, it was women and children alone who benefit from these miracles. The single exception is that of a man cured from impotency: 'who had been lately married, but who through magic art could not consort with his wife; but when they [the family] had passed that night with him, his bond was loosed'. And on the morrow the husband, as well he might have done, made a great feast for them.

Miracles of a more terrestrial nature have their places in this curious period: Mary gives Jesus a water jar and sends him to draw water, 'but the boy being thronged by the press of people at the well, the pot was broken. But Jesus spread out the garment with which he was clothed and filling it with water, carried it to his mother'. She was still in constant attendance on him, and closely associated with almost every one of the events of this period in her son's life; but on one occasion when 'Jesus was eight year old', he 'went out with his father to sow corn in their field, and when his father sowed, the

75 The family are given lodgings in the palace of Prince Alsamander Porlac; Jesus is taking his first steps between Mary and Joseph; in the opening is the Old Testament Joseph riding in triumph. By Providone, c. 1695.

child Jesus also sowed one grain of corn. And having reaped and threshed it, he made a hundred quarters of it. And having called all the poor of the village to the threshing floor, he bestowed the corn on them'; and 'Joseph took a little for a blessing from Jesus to his house'. This field was shown to the pilgrim Antoninus of Placentia in about the year 570. He was told that it yielded two crops a year, the first of which was gathered miraculously in February, and served to make the holy wafers for the Easter Communion, whereas the second was harvested at the normal season with the rest of the crop; after which, he reports, 'the field was plowed'.

There is still another class of miracle, which need not detain us, of the man-into-donkey, woman-into-mule type, in which we too easily see Arabian glosses, or smell a little too strongly the odour of Ahriman the Persian Lucifer who was sometimes as much a prankster as the Evil One. Occasionally there is a more rational gleam in the text and on one occasion the child, with his companions, seems to be playing that old game called 'King of the Castle'. But the Arabic Gospel, from which we have drawn most of these strange stories, must have suffered, in the condition in which we know it, emendation after emendation and addition after addition, until it became the most imperfect of the books with which we have to deal. Others, such as the various versions of Thomas' Gospel, or Pseudo-Matthew, do little to help our knowledge of the events, or of the proper side of Jesus' nature at this time. They give less space to Jesus' miracles; but while those of every period of his childhood require a greater or lesser effort of suspension of disbelief, all the writings dealing with the good deeds of this period are preoccupied with happenings which have more in them of magic than divinity. It is an unsatisfactory time in the history of the young Jesus. But it is also the time of his 'Malevolent Acts', which are treated separately in the next chapter; and it is they which may be considered to be the dominating feature of the life of the Holy Family in Egypt.

opposite above
76 Jesus strikes down and kills the boy who ran against his shoulder. From a French manuscript, fifteenth century.

opposite below
77 The complaining neighbours are struck blind (their eyes are closed, indicating blindness). From a French manuscript, fifteenth century.

overleaf
78 Jesus turns the village children into pigs. From an English Book of Hours, fourteenth century.

10 The malevolent acts of Jesus

Here we have to consider a series of acts by the youthful Jesus over which, as some would maintain, it might be better to draw a prudent veil. They are of such a character that their commission—if, indeed, we are to believe that they ever occurred—denotes a child who is at certain times a hardened delinquent: arrogant, ruthless and homicidal. In this chapter a single facet of the biblical character of Jesus will be examined: some of these stories will be set out in full and we shall very briefly examine their background and their history, insofar as this is possible at the distance of time which separates us from them; and finally we shall show something of the tenacity with which these tales have been remembered through all the Christian centuries, and until quite modern times.

These acts themselves, of course, are apocryphal. There is no trace of them—any more than there is a trace of any other aspect of Jesus' childhood—in the canon. The man, the Jesus of the Evangelists, we know: the kind, the wise, the great, the all-powerful; and the hot-tempered and the cunning. A character of many facets. We shall have more to say later on the composition of these Gospels, but even as we know them today it could be maintained that amongst so much that is whole they show a flaw in the temperament of Jesus: a flaw in his attitude towards Joseph and Mary, and his brothers and sisters. We should remember that on that Friday which was to be the beginning of the first Easter, Mary his mother came to the execution ground to witness with anguish and horror the death of her son: and that he, in his agony, committed her into the care of the disciple whom he most loved. This act, carried out *in extremis*, and recorded only in the

overleaf
79 Jesus walks up a sunbeam: his companions try to emulate him, but fall and break their pates. From an English Book of Hours, fourteenth century.

opposite
80 With a gesture, Jesus turns the husbandman's seed corn to stones. From a French manuscript, fifteenth century.

Gospel of John, is the sole, the only passage in the whole of the New Testament in which Jesus may be said to have shown concern for any member of his immediate family.

Luke tells us that even as a child of twelve, he had slipped away from the group with which Mary and Joseph were returning from their annual attendance at the Passover at Jerusalem. After long searching, they found him again in the company of the Doctors of the Temple, but he gave them no other welcome than *How is it that you sought me? Wist ye not that I must be about my Father's business?* When, years later, he went out to begin his ministry he appears already to have cut any ties which might have united him with his father and mother, his brothers and sisters. Only three days after his baptism in Jordan when, according to John, his mother Mary was present at the marriage of Cana, and spoke to him, he rounds on her with *Woman, what have I to do with thee? mine hour is not yet come.* He accepted more distant relatives into his immediate circle; but it is not recorded that he even visited his parent's home when he went into his own district of Nazareth where, a too-familiar figure as a local carpenter and a local carpenter's son, he found that as a prophet he could expect *no honour in his own country.* And when, in a house in Galilee, he was told that his mother and his brethren were without desiring to speak to him, he answers *Who is my mother? and who are my brethren?* and will not receive them, holding his disciples alone, and his close followers, to be his only family on earth.

Apart from the 'Birth' stories at the beginning of Matthew and Luke, these are the only references in the whole of the Gospels to Mary, or to Joseph. Joseph, of course, is an inconvenient figure, and he disappears entirely from view after the Passover visit to Jerusalem save for one brief reference to a carpenter. But the brief appearances of Mary, and of the brothers and sisters, could be thought of as a foil against which to set off Jesus' rejection of earthly bonds; and this posture might have been accepted in an anchorite, a man of the desert. But Jesus was not a hermit, setting himself apart from the world and all its works. He was an orator and a teacher who sought to convert all men to his beliefs, an itinerant preacher who sat with publicans and sinners, a man jostled by the crowds who came to see and hear him, who performed miracles in the sight of all and who had close and devoted followers among both men and women. He was a man of the world; and this sharp denial of his parents and his family, and his call to others to deny their families as he had done, must have appeared not only singular, but exaggerated, abnormal, in the context of a patriarchal Jewish society, one of whose major strengths had always been its close-knit family groups.

This conscious rejection of all filial ties may provide us with a possible clue to the meaning of this mysterious and alarming group of stories which have come down to us and which, as we have said, show us in a single period of his childhood an altogether un-looked-for aspect of the character of Jesus. But first we must examine the framework of the stories, and the stories themselves. We have already settled the holy Family, for their sojourn in Egypt, in Materea; and it seems reasonably safe to assume that they spent at least five, and possibly seven years in that town. During this exile, then, the child who had left Palestine at two years old grew into a young boy; and while, at times, he continued to perform beneficent acts, this other, this malevolent side of his character appeared. He set out, in fact, on a series of actions which are entirely alien from his normal pattern of behaviour, and it is not too much to say that once he had broken away from his mother's apron strings he became nearer to a monster than a God. We have seen that his biblical relationship with his parents was not by any means that of a dutiful son; but now, in this special period of his life in Egypt, he escapes from their control, abuses them, and embarks on a series of violent and reprehensible acts which bring them to shame and almost to a yet more distant exile.

The tradition of these, which are generally called the 'Malevolent' acts of Jesus, was widespread in the ancient world and most of them are set out in substantially the same form in all the major apocryphal writings of the 'Infancy' group, save only for the Protevangelium, which goes no further than the 'Birth' scenes and the murder of Zacharias. It is almost impossible, today, to speculate on the true origins of these disturbing stories, but their existence in the earliest Christian centuries may owe something, not only to the widespread Gnosticism of the time, but to the influence of Zoroastrianism, with its insistence on the coaeval, co-existent and balanced forces of good and evil. To later Christians, the stories should have been—and were— anathema. Yet, as the illustrations to this chapter show, a precise knowledge of them in unaltered form, save for an occasional gloss of piety, an additional act of redress, persisted throughout Western Europe until the very end of the Middle Ages. And we shall see that echoes of them were still to be heard much later: even in England, even into modern times.

At this 'malevolent' period of his boyhood, Jesus seemed at first to find his amusements, like any other small town boy, in running about the streets, paddling in the streams and wandering in the fields, sometimes—at least, in the early days, before they had learnt better—with the neighbour's children. But though he was sometimes with them, he was not of them, for he was a child set apart, one who had within him supernatural gifts which could both create and destroy. As a growing boy his play with his companions, when it was not actually dangerous to them, was shot with malice, and his arrogant and casual superiority to all around him would have been, in a normal child, shocking to a degree. But he was an abnormal child, and in this special case, at this special time, a greater power led to a greater evil: he began to use the miraculous and beneficent attributes, which he demonstrated with such effect as an infant, in the manner of one who has total prerogatives and total jurisdiction untempered by responsibility or pity. Those who cross him, or offend him in any way, are struck blind, or 'withered', or changed in shape. Or they simply drop dead at his command.

81 Joseph and Mary threatened by their neighbours. Wall-tile from Tring Parish Church, Hertfordshire, England, early fourteenth century.

We can take our first example of these extraordinary manifestations from an incident which seems to have occurred in the earlier days of the exile in Egypt. Jesus was walking down the street when a lad, running towards him, knocked against his shoulder. The 'malevolent' character of Jesus seems already to have been established, for in the words of the Infancy Gospel of Thomas:

> 76
> Jesus was exasperated and said to the lad, You shall go no further on your way, and the child immediately fell down and died. But some, who saw what took place, said: From whence does this child spring, since his every word is an accomplished deed? And the parents of the dead child came to Joseph and blamed
> 81
> him and said: Since you have such a child, you cannot dwell with us in the village; or else teach him to bless and not to curse. For he is slaying our children. And Joseph called the child aside and admonished him, saying: Why do you do such things that these people must suffer and hate and persecute us? But Jesus replied, I know that these words are not yours; nevertheless for your sake I will be silent. But they shall bear their punishment. And immediately those that had accused him
> 77
> became blind. And those who saw it were greatly afraid and perplexed, and said concerning him: Every word he speaks, whether good or evil, was a deed and became a marvel!

A terrifying, an evil, a miraculous act has happened. In the illustrations to the tale as it was still told in a late fifteenth-century manuscript it will be seen that a tardy retribution was made, the blind restored to sight, and the boy to life; but it was not always thus, and in the early texts these deeds are generally allowed to stand. A later passage in Thomas' Gospel speaks of the healing of all who had been 'maimed' by the boy's curses, but it is by no means clear that this is a blanket retribution covering this dead lad.

Petulance, in the child Jesus of these stories, takes monstrous forms. On another occasion, a group of boys with whom he had sometimes played in the past were running in the street while their parents, in the cool of the evening, were sitting in their doorways. By now, they had seen more than enough of the character and capabilities of Jesus, and they would do anything in their power to prevent their children from crossing his path; so that when they heard that he was coming their way, they were terrified and cast about them for a place to conceal their young. It would seem that their own houses were not proof against his magical powers, and in their panic they hit upon the idea of the communal oven as a hiding place, and quickly bundling the children

82 Jesus turns the village children into pigs, a dramatic two-part scene from the Holkham Bible Picture Book, second quarter of the fourteenth century.

82 inside, closed the doors on them. Jesus arrived on the scene and, with an appearance of innocence—for he is all-knowing and understands perfectly what he is about, and what has been done to thwart him—asked, 'Where are all the children?' The fearful parents said that they did not know; that they were not there; that they had been away for a long time and would soon be back, for they must surely be playing in the fields outside the town. 'Very well', Jesus said, 'but what is in the oven which I see here?' 'Inside', said the parents, 'there's just some suckling pigs dressed for roasting.' 'So be it', Jesus replied, 'let them be pigs'. And he went on his way. The terrified parents rushed to the oven *78 82* and threw open the doors. And inside, of course, there was nothing but piglets.

There are variants to this sinister story. In the 'Arabic' Gospel the piglets became young goats which, when the doors were opened, jumped out of the oven and skipped about at the feet of those who had been their parents. Sometimes the metamorphosed children, in the form of pigs, or kidlets, are actually found to be cooked and ready to be eaten. And sometimes the intercession of Mary, who in at least the later versions of some of these stories calls upon her son for pity for his victims, is successful and the children are allowed to resume their former shape. But even if this were to be accepted as a happy conclusion to this affair of sorcery, the fact remains that the all-powerful boy has been shown to us as being capable of a gratuitous act of cruelty which has brought terror and anguish to neighbouring families which, as far as we know, were innocent of any crime against him.

The child of these stories has become monstrously unpredictable and, save only occasionally by his mother, ungovernable. We should consider the following passage, which is quoted directly from the Gospel of Pseudo-Matthew in Harris Cowper's translation, and which, moreover, appears in substantially the same form both in Thomas and in the Arabic Gospel: Jesus is playing by the river, at the water's edge, and other children are near him. 'Jesus made himself seven pools with mud, to each of which he made little channels through which, at his bidding, he brought water from the stream into the pools, and sent it back again. Then one of the children, the son of the Devil, and of an envious mind, shut up the channels which supplied water to the pools, and overthrew what Jesus had made. Then said Jesus unto him, Woe unto thee, son of death, son of Satan. Dost thou destroy the works which I have wrought? And straightway he who had done this died. Then, with a quarrelsome voice, the parents of the dead cried out against Mary and Joseph, saying to them, Your son has cursed our son, and he is dead. When Joseph and Mary heard, they came at once to Jesus, on account of the complaints of the boy, and the crowd of townspeople. But Joseph said secretly to Mary, I dare not speak to him; but do thou admonish him, and say, Why hast thou raised against us the enmity of the people, and why must we hear the painful enmity of men? And when his mother had come to him, she asked him, saying, My Lord, what hath he done that he should die? But he said, He was worthy of death, because he destroyed the works which I had wrought. Therefore his mother besought him, saying, Do not, my Lord, because they all rise against us. And he, not willing that his mother should be grieved, spurned the body with his right foot, and said to him, Arise, O son of iniquity, for thou art not worthy to enter into the rest of my Father, because thou hast destroyed the works which I have wrought. Then the dead arose and departed. But Jesus, at his own command, brought water into the pools through the water-channels.'

In this murderous, magical episode which set the whole township by the ears and which raised the mob against the exiles and their child, Mary's intercession, though it seems to have been made more through fear than through compassion, was successful, and the dead boy, with a rough gesture and unforgiving words, was brought back to life. But in many other lethal incidents, Jesus showed neither pity nor remorse for his acts. Knowing what would happen, he walked on the water and cynically urged his companions to follow him. They did so, of course,

ne autrefoiz marie et io
seph furent deprrez du
peuple quilz envoiassent
ihus a lescolle pour apn
dre. et ilz ny refuserent
pas Mais lenuoierent

and were 'drowned all'. Or he built a bridge across a ravine 'with the beams of the sun' and walked over it, calling on his companions to do the same. Foolishly, they tried to cross over in their turn and fell to their deaths. As we have seen, he once sowed wheat in time of dearth with his own hands, and it bore a thousand-fold, so that all the town was fed; but on another occasion he came upon a man sowing his field and without reason, or explanation, or eventual redress, he turned his seed corn to stones.

79 84

80

The last example which we shall give of these 'Malevolent Acts' is the story of 'Jesus and the Schoolmasters', with its curious echoes of the biblical story of the Doctors in the Temple who were *astonished at his understanding and answers*. It reads in this way in the Gospel of Thomas:

> Joseph, seeing the understanding of the child, and that he was growing tall, and becoming a youth, considered again that he should not remain unacquainted with letters. So he took him, and handed him over to another teacher, who said to Joseph, I will first instruct the child in Greek, and then in Hebrew; for the teacher knew the cleverness of the child, and was afraid of him. Nevertheless, he wrote out the alphabet, and repeated it to him for a long time, but his pupil remained silent. At last Jesus said: If you are indeed a teacher, and know the letters properly yourself, tell me the power of Alpha, and I will tell you the power of Beta. At this, the teacher became angry, and struck Jesus on the head; whereat the child became enraged, and cursed him. Immediately, the teacher fell down senseless and died. And Jesus left the school, and went home. When Joseph learned what had happened, he wept bitterly and charged the child's mother to keep him closely within doors for, he said, all who provoked him, died.

83

In some apocryphal books, Jesus has as many as three teachers successively, but this man with his Greek is the only one among them who actually strikes Jesus, and dies for his temerity. The others, who imprudently checked or scolded him for his arrogance, had no more than narrow escapes; and when the child is allowed to hold forth freely and to astonish his audience with his learning, his spirits are excellent, and he is inclined to resuscitate, and to forgive, all those whom he has struck down so casually.

83 The teacher falls dead, clutching the hand which he had dared to lift against Jesus. From a French manuscript, fifteenth century.

As we have seen elsewhere, there are occasions when the apocryphals parallel the Evangelists; and even at this 'Malevolent' period of Jesus' life, acts of charity, and forgiveness, and healing, in which the child is truly father to the man, are interspersed in the texts with these tales of malice, which themselves have no parallels whatever in the canon, and only their faint shadow in that fig tree of Bethany which has worried so many Christians. On the other hand, it has been suggested at the beginning of this chapter that the canonical passages concerning Jesus' relationship with his family demonstrate a one who is less than perfect; yet they have been allowed to stand, for reasons which are no longer apparent to us, in three of the four Gospels as we know them. It is not an unreasonable hypothesis to suppose that some of the much more disturbing tales which have been grouped together here may have been known to those figures, so shadowy to us, who were the Evangelists, and may even have appeared, in one form or another, in their original writings; only to be prudently edited out from those rather late texts of the Gospels which are all that are available to us today. Had they, on the other hand, remained in the canon, they would have been the subject of endless analysis and debate and would eventually have been rationalised in the same way that generations not long past, who maintained the infallibility of the entire biblical text, rationalised the positive contradictions of the birth stories of Matthew and Luke, and wedded them together in an apparently harmonious whole.

This is not an irrational supposition, nor should it shock. Given the curious history of the selection and bringing together of the New Testament canon, and the acceptance of Gospel records which, having their origins in widely scattered parts of the Mediterranean, show the divergencies—and sometimes the marked divergencies—of different times and traditions, speculation on the details of the original form and content of the Gospels is not only an allowable exercise, but one which has been indulged in for centuries. The apocryphal writings for their part, have not been subject to anything approaching the same intense exegesis. But what is certain is that the first written records of these explicitly 'Malevolent' acts emerge from the mists of the first Christian centuries; that their origins are embedded in very ancient Christian texts of a generally pietistic content; that their substance was known throughout Christendom, from North to South and from East to West, for at least a millennium and a half; and that they cannot be ignored when apocryphal texts are discussed, or artifacts arising from them examined.

Throughout recorded history miracles and wonders, by no means necessarily beneficent, have been part and parcel of religious belief, and the world has been finely balanced between the influence of the Divine and the powers of Evil. To recent generations, little given to the sophistications of theology, it has seemed blasphemous even to consider that the character of Jesus might have its flaws, that a God of Anger might be a facet of a God of Mercy. Jesus, to the general, is an indistinctly observed perfection. Nevertheless, these stories of that other, youthful aspect—which the apocryphals themselves attribute to his childhood, and only to his childhood—are rooted in textual history, have been rooted in human memory, and have never quite died. On the side of the normal, the 'beneficent' nature, we have seen the miracle of the Palm Tree turned, for northern voices and northern understandings, into the carol of the 'Cherry Tree', which is sung in many tongues; and the story of the miracle of the Wheatfield living on in England, in all its details, in the song of 'The Carnal and the Crane'. On the other hand,

84 Jesus walks on the water and beckons to his companions to follow him: they do, and drown; and trying to follow Jesus up a sunbeam, they fall. They clash pots with him, and their pot breaks. From the Holkham Bible Picture Book, second quarter of the fourteenth century.

certainly as late as the seventeenth century, and almost certainly much later still, and even in Britain, which was for so long on the outer edges of an earlier Christendom, a carol such as 'The Bitter Withy' was still current. In this song Jesus asks some boys to play at ball with him. They answer that they are lords' and ladies' sons, and will have nothing to do with the likes of him:

> . . . Then at the last I'll make it appear
>   That I am above you all.'

> Our Saviour built a bridge with the beams of the sun
>   And over he gone, he gone he;
> And after followed the jolly jerdins,
>   And drowndèd they were all three.

> It was upling scorn and downling scorn!
>   The mothers of them did whoop and call,
> Crying out, 'Mary mild, call home your child,
>   For ours are drowndèd all!'

> Mary mild, Mary mild called home her child,
>   And laid our Saviour across her knee,
> And with a whole handful of bitter withy,
>   She gave him slashes three.

> Then he said to his mother: 'Oh! the withy! oh the withy!
>   The bitter withy that causes me to smart, to smart,
> Oh the withy shall be the very first tree
>   That perishes at the heart!'

This is almost certainly a bowdlerised version of an earlier original, and two 'Malevolent' tales are here confused. But the song shows how very long they are in dying, these stories of a boy whose arrogance and anger could become miraculous and terrible, the obverse face of the majestic deeds of his manhood.

11 *The return to Nazareth*

86   *But when Herod was dead, behold, an angel of the Lord appeareth in a dream to Joseph in Egypt,*
Saying, Arise, and take the young child and his mother, and go into the land of Israel: for they are dead which sought the young child's life.
And he arose, and took the young child and his mother, and came into the land of Israel.
85   *But when he heard that Archelaus did reign in Judaea in the room of his father Herod, he was afraid to go thither: notwithstanding, being warned of God in a dream, he turned aside into the parts of Galilee.*
And he came and dwelt in a city called Nazareth: that it might be fulfilled which was spoken by the prophets, He shall be called a Nazarene.

In the context of Matthew's extremely succinct story of the birth and the earliest years of Jesus' life, this is a comprehensive statement of events; and indeed it contains most of what we know of the actual return from Egypt. The major 'Infancy' apocryphals, by and large, are silent on the subject, for by now Jesus is a growing lad of nine or perhaps even ten years old, and their job is done. There is, or was, a view that at least five of the chapters of the Arabic Gospel applied to this period, but it is difficult to maintain that the author or authors of the work set down events in an ordered sequence, and any matters of interest in that part of the work, save for one incident which clearly seems to refer to the journey back, have been given to the Egyptian period. Fortunately, we can learn a little more of the life of the Family after they had returned to Nazareth, and we gather more adult and 'masculine' information than hitherto—though all of it is suspect—which provides us, among other things, with at least some information on the life of Joseph as a man and a carpenter.

There is, then, little solid information concerning this return. The 'History of the Virgin Mary as told by herself to Timothy, Patriarch of Alexandria', an Ethiopian work of which we have late copies, purports to record the return from Egypt, but its matter is heavily overlaid with pagan magic dressed up in Christian form. According to this 'History', the Holy Family wished to go by sea from Egypt to Palestine; and setting out from 'a town filled with thorn bushes' they reached a port during a great storm, which Jesus duly quelled. Nevertheless, none of the boatmasters in the harbour was willing to carry them; but the great rock on which they were sitting at the time moved of its own accord out to sea and towards their destination. This magical rock, however, was the property of a powerful sorceress, who, when she heard that it had fallen into the hands of Jesus, sent legions of her devils 'to bring them [the family] to her in chains'; and when her minions failed to do so she pursued them herself in a great sea-chariot which Jesus destroyed by his superior power. After further adventures they reached their landfall and it was here, in this particular story, that they had their encounter with the robbers who eventually suffered at the Crucifixion. But the Abyssinian imagination in these matters was always extensive, and we should do better to assume that the Holy Family travelled by land throughout, and that they used the more convenient coastal road, for with the divine assurance and direction which had come to them they could not think that they would meet any major obstacles on the way or, with Herod dead, that they would be in any danger from the civil power.

Paintings often show both Mary and Jesus mounted for the return journey, with only Joseph continuing to trudge along on foot. Traditionally, Mary is riding the same ass which carried her on the outward journey: Jesus is mounted on its foal. But sometimes there is only one animal, and then a hierarchical view was often taken of the order of march with the little Lord, already a strapping fellow, riding the beast while his parents, on foot, follow behind, or cling to the stirrup leathers. Salome, in spite of her protestations of life-long fidelity, is seldom shown as being with them on this long march, and she seems to have drifted out of the story; though the genealogy maintained by the Abyssinian church held that not only was she Mary's willing bondmaid, but her cousin, the daughter of a Mary who was Anne's sister, and also the cousin of Elizabeth, who was held to be the daughter of a third sister called Sophia. For the Ethiopians with their intense Marialism, it was unthinkable that the Mother of God, generatrix of miracles on this earth and the intercessionary vehicle for salvation in the next, would ever be deserted. In one of the hagiographies of their diffuse and quarrelsome church it is held that 'St' Salome stayed with the Mother of Jesus throughout the Flight and through all the days of her later life and—at a time in history when the doctrine of the 'Assumption' had

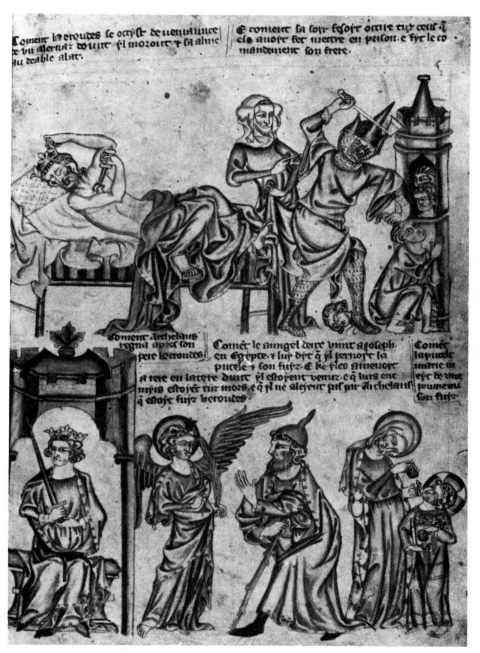

Comment heroudes se ocrist de menaunce
le vn merual tourut sil moroitt. t sa alme
au deable alat.

E coment sa soer sesoit ocrre tuz ceus q
els auoit fer mettre en prison. e hyt le co
manndement son frere.

coment Archelaus
regna aprel son
frere heroudes

Comet le aungel duit uiut a ioseph
en Egipte. t luy dist q il pernoyt sa
pucele t son fuyz. E he sles amenoit
a tere en latere duit il estoient venir. e q lurs ene
mys estoient tuz mors. e q il ne alerent pas par Archelaus
q estoit fuyz heroudes

Comet
lapucele
marie in
ecfe de vne
poume ou
son fuyz

85 In this version of the story, Herod commits suicide and his sister, at his orders, has
the prisoners killed. Below, Archelaus reigns in his stead; the angel tells Joseph that
Herod is dead and that Archelaus is king; and Mary gives Jesus the apple of Eden (see
Chapter 12). From the Holkham Bible Picture Book, second quarter of the fourteenth
century.

The house of Herod

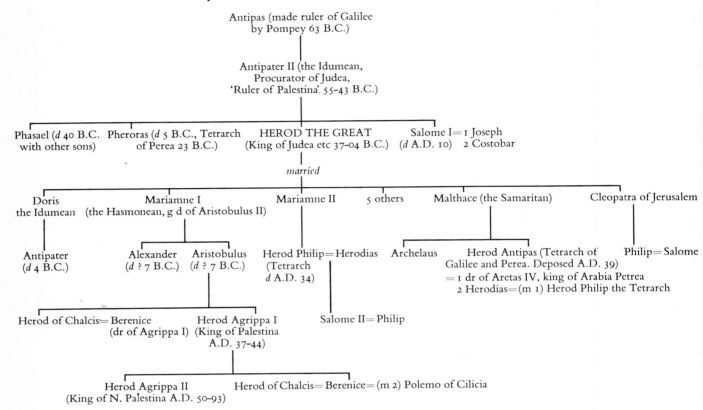

Antipas (made ruler of Galilee
by Pompey 63 B.C.)

Antipater II (the Idumean,
Procurator of Judea,
'Ruler of Palestina'. 55-43 B.C.)

Phasael (*d* 40 B.C.   Pheroras (*d* 5 B.C., Tetrarch   HEROD THE GREAT   Salome I= 1 Joseph
with other sons)   of Perea 23 B.C.)   (King of Judea etc 37-04 B.C.)   (*d* A.D. 10)   2 Costobar

married

Doris   Mariamne I   Mariamne II   5 others   Malthace (the Samaritan)   Cleopatra of Jerusalem
the Idumean   (the Hasmonean, g d of Aristobulus II)

Antipater   Alexander   Aristobulus   Herod Philip=Herodias   Archelaus   Herod Antipas (Tetrarch of   Philip= Salome
(*d* 4 B.C.)   (*d* ? 7 B.C.)   (*d* ? 7 B.C.)   (Tetrarch   Galilee and Perea. Deposed A.D. 39)
     d A.D. 34)   = 1 dr of Aretas IV, king of Arabia Petrea
     2 Herodias=(m 1) Herod Philip the Tetrarch

Herod of Chalcis= Berenice   Herod Agrippa I   Salome II= Philip
(dr of Agrippa I)   (King of Palestina
A.D. 37-44)

Herod Agrippa II   Herod of Chalcis= Berenice=(m 2) Polemo of Cilicia
(King of N. Palestina A.D. 50-93)

not yet reached the authors of the tale — that she was with her at the end, performing the last rites, and burying her with the help of hosts of angels.

    Surprisingly the news of Archelaus's succession does not seem to have reached Joseph in Materea, for it was not until he crossed the border from Egypt and came to the land of Israel. that he learnt, from the fourth and last of those dreams whereby Matthew presses on the action, that he *did reign in Judea in the room of his father Herod.*

opposite
86 A purulent, disintegrating Herod, consumed by the shades of the slaughtered Innocents. By Guiseppe Arcimboldo, who perfected the painting of 'composed heads' such as this, and worked for the Habsburg Court in Prague and Vienna in 1565–87.

overleaf
87 The return from Egypt — Jesus rides the donkey. From an Italian manuscript, fourteenth century.

vtat̄ q̄ amatioms ꝛ ſimłr faciũt Nec nūī
ueꝛdat̄ q̄ fiłi. venitam hūiłr. ḡ eis eḡ Vo
ꝑati potes cū ille cui ē tīa ꝛpłetu̅ do ei̅ ꝑſe
nutio ſuo · ſic pauꝑtate̅ artā elegēt vn̄ īta

86   Joseph feared this new king, and he was right to do so. A senile Herod, in making the last of his many wills, had divided his dominions between his remaining sons; but he had narrowed his own choice, and Archelaus would not normally have inherited Judea. A few years before this time, his best-loved sons Alexander and Aristobulus had been receiving a princely education at the imperial court of Rome, where Augustus Caesar, who had always been their father's friend, had favoured them exceedingly; but the two young men, on their mother's side, were descended from the old Hasmonean royal house which still counted many loyalties among the Jews and their mother, Mariamne I, had been murdered by their father. They owed him little loyalty. Herod suspected, not without reason, that they were plotting to overthrow him and to seize his throne before their time, and the crazed old king had them

85   brought back to Palestine and executed, a deed which he afterwards regretted almost as much as he had regretted his insensate killing of Mariamne, who had been, it was said, one of the most beautiful women of her time. And now, after a succession of household murders, Judea, and the difficult Samaria, had become Archelaus' heritage and two years after the death of his half-brothers he succeeded to the throne of Jerusalem. In the ten years of his reign, he showed himself to be so dissolute a man and so brutal and avaricious a king that the Romans, tolerant as they usually were of such characteristics in their client kings on the fringes of Empire, had little choice but to forestall an actual revolt in the province by deposing him. In the event, Archelaus was lucky and escaped with his life, which he ended in comfortable exile on the Rhine, but his sordid misrule, which had brought the country to a state of anarchy, precipitated the end of Palestine as a semi-independent state. But while this man was still the ruler of Judea, Joseph had every reason to avoid this troubled country and to turn aside *into the parts of Galilee* where another Herod was king. For Matthew, who had seemed to be directing them back to the Bethlehem whence they came, this would have meant a change of homeland, almost another exile; but in the Lukan tradition they are going back to their own home.

    To avoid Archelaus's territory and to reach Galilee in reasonable

overleaf
88 Mary finds Jesus again in the Temple with the Doctors. Stained glass window by Hans Acker in Ulm Cathedral, Germany, fifteenth century.

opposite
89 Jesus in the dyer's shop: 1. The cloths waiting to be dyed. 2. He puts them all in the same vat. 3. The cloths come out in the required colours. From an English manuscript, *c.* 1300.

safety, he would have had to follow the southern borders of Judea, and then to turn northwards along the east coast of the Dead Sea and the left bank of the Jordan, which would have had the additional advantage of avoiding an unfriendly Samaria. On this road, on the Jordan, there occurred the only significant miracle-story of the journey which is recorded in the apocryphals. A multitude of people, in this singular tale, had come out to see them and Jesus was strolling at his ease on the banks of the river, accompanied by a group of lions known for their particular savagery, but which, nevertheless, he had rendered docile and debonair, so that their cubs gambolled about his feet as he walked. And 'in the sight of all the people there gathered Jesus crossed the river with the lions and their whelps, for the waters made a wall to them on their right hand and on their left'. In this tale a new, a greater Moses showed his power to the assembled populace who, mindful as they always were of the history of their race, would have quickly taken the point. We know no more of this journey, though there is a tradition that on the road to Galilee the family visited Jerusalem. The scene is not infrequently shown in mediaeval artifacts, but this particular 'visit', which rests on no text known to us, was probably a late invention designed to increase still further the sanctity of the Holy City by adding to its roll of honour another connection with Jesus at yet another period of his life. Very few, after all, knew Matthew's Gospel, or the reasons which Joseph had for skirting the Judea of Archelaus, and it was easy, and advantageous in mediaeval times, to add Jerusalem to the itinerary of the return from Egypt.

So the little group came home again to Nazareth and were reunited with their family and friends. According to an Ethiopic story Joseph was set up again in his calling by another carpenter called Delanos who settled them into their home and brought them certain 'necessities', which one may assume to be the tools of the trade. By now, as we have seen, Jesus would have been about ten years old and presumably was already at work, helping his father. It was two years later, or perhaps a little more, in the spring when he was twelve, that the Holy Family made that particular visit to Jerusalem which Luke has celebrated in a dozen verses and with a masterly economy of words. We find ourselves again on firmer ground:

> Now his parents went to Jerusalem every year at the feast of the passover.
> And when he was twelve years old, they went up to Jerusalem, after the custom of the feast.
> And when they had fulfilled the days, as they returned, the child Jesus tarried behind in Jerusalem; and Joseph and his mother knew not of it.

But they, supposing him to have been in the company, went a day's journey; and they sought him among their kinsfolk and acquaintances.

And when they found him not, they turned back again to Jerusalem, seeking him.

88 *And it came to pass, that after three days they found him in the temple, sitting in the midst of the doctors, both hearing them, and asking them questions.*

And all that heard him were astonished at his understanding and answers.

And when they saw him, they were amazed: and his mother said unto him, Son, why hast thou thus dealt with us? Behold, thy father and I have sought thee sorrowing.

And he said unto them, How is it that ye sought me? Wist ye not that I must be about my father's business?

And they understood not the saying which he spake unto them.

90 *And he went down with them, and came to Nazareth, and was subject unto them: but his mother kept all these sayings in her heart.*

And Jesus increased in wisdom and stature, and in favour with God and man.

The implications of this trip to Jerusalem are as interesting as the story itself. When the great Temple, the heart of the faith, was still standing every Jewish family would have wished to do as Joseph's did, for their presence at Jerusalem at the Passover was a sanctification, a festival and a holiday in the true sense of that word. But the distance which they would have had to travel from Nazareth to Jerusalem, along the route which they would have taken down the valley of the Jordan, was about 120 miles; and with women and children in the party, and a week at least to be spent in the Holy City, the trip can hardly have taken much less than a month. At these times of high festival, with many families converging on Jerusalem from every part of Palestine and from all the Jewish colonies overseas, prices were likely to have been high on the road, and particularly high in Jerusalem. The trip, however simply it might have been carried out, would have been an expensive one, and for Jesus' family to have undertaken it every year shows that they were people of some substance. We have no certain knowledge of their material circumstances, but on the evidence of Luke's Gospel alone we must suppose that they had 13 possessions—as we believe from other sources that they had a vineyard —and that Joseph, the carpenter, was a successful artisan in a comfortable way of business. They travelled to Jerusalem in a group with their *kinsfolk and acquaintance,* who must themselves have been in a position to make the journey, so that it would seem that in Nazareth they lived in a circle of the *petite bourgeoisie*, comfortably off, with bondsmen and servants about them. And a goodly company they must have made in that spring of the year, with the great crowd of friends and neighbours on the road together, and so many children wandering from one end to the other of the long caravan: so many that on the return journey it was a whole day before Joseph and Mary realised that Jesus was not among them.

In telling us this single story of Jesus' boyhood—the only one to be found in the Gospels—Luke is providing a framework for the visit to the Doctors of the Temple and, in this 'Jewish' passage of his Gospel, he is drawing our attention to the precocity of Jesus at twelve year's old. Since early times the Jewish people have held scholarship in profound respect, with theological scholarship the highest of their disciplines. The material and mystical exegesis of the Mosaic Torah was the chief preoccupation of the priests and 'Doctors' of the Temple in Jesus' day as, with the weighty addition of the Talmud, it is today among the ministering body of the faith. Even a modest degree of proficiency in the art can only be attained by long study and reflection; and Luke is emphasising the remarkable attainments of Jesus as a young boy. The non-Jewish Christians were, almost without exception, poor and unlettered men, with no tradition of learning. Here, Luke is not addressing himself to them, but is showing us the scholar who will merit the love and respect of his own race.

83 The 'schoolmaster' episodes—where Jesus knows more than his teachers—which occur in Pseudo-Matthew and others, and which we have seen elsewhere, are part of this same tradition of juvenile scholarship. Similarly, the earliest Greek text of Thomas's apocryphal Gospel gives Luke's brief story of the Doctors of the Temple, adding that the twelve-year-old Jesus stood among the 'elders and teachers of the people', amazing them with his precocity and 'resolving the heads of the law and the parables of the prophets'. The Arabic Gospel pushes the theme to remarkable lengths: here, true to the Persian overtones of the book, Jesus not only astonishes the Temple elders, but also a 'philosopher skilled in astronomy' and a 'doctor of medicine'. To the astronomer he expounded the nature of the celestial bodies, and their operations, to the 'sixtieths of degrees'; and to the doctor he explained physics and metaphysics, the humours of the body, its bones, veins, arteries and nerves—and much else besides—and expounded the operation of the soul on the body, and its senses, and virtues, 'with many other things which the intellect of no creature attains unto'. Persian erudition spread its net wider than its Jewish counterpart, and all was applied to Jesus. But in the West a precocious child has seldom been generally admired. The many pictures which show the scene of

Jesus' discussions with the Doctors in the Temple often have anti-Semitic overtones, and almost always illustrate the moment when Mary makes her appearance among the company. In the hagiography of a church with strong Marialist leanings and a generally indifferent scholarship Luke's story has tended to be considered as a framework, not for Jesus' intellectual brilliance, but for one of the 'Seven Sorrows of Mary' when she had lost her child and for one of her 'Seven Joys' when she found him again. Here, as elsewhere, the Gospel is politicised and bent to a prevailing theology.

It is unlikely that the Nazareth caravan would have waited five days for Joseph and Mary, and we can assume that when the family was reunited they returned home alone. There, Jesus was 'subject' to his parents, under unspecified conditions. He found 'favour with God and man' but whether this included the members of his own family is uncertain. At twelve years old, he had rebelled and disappeared, quite clearly intending to leave them and to find his own way in the world. Parental authority had compelled him to return to his own home, and Luke has no more to say on the matter; but in the nature of things we should have expected this exceptional child, now growing into adolescence, to break out again from the parental bonds. The early non-canonical material does not enlighten us on the real relationships within the family; but as we should expect, it has Jesus operating on a different, a higher and more powerful plane than Joseph and Mary.

90 Jesus 'subject' to his parents: he draws water, freshens up the fire and serves at table. From the Holkham Bible Picture Book, second quarter of the fourteenth century.

We have seen that the family was well-to-do in a modest way, and Joseph probably a good master-carpenter; but it was necessary for the apocryphals to show that Jesus was a better one than he, and that even in joinery he could work miracles. Pseudo-Matthew had it that Joseph made 'yokes for oxen, and ploughs and implements for turning up the soil and suited for agriculture, and wooden bedsteads'; and with one of these bedsteads, made for 'a certain youth' Jesus performed a miracle which is given a far more picturesque framework in the Arabic Gospel. There, it is said that 'all men sent for him [Joseph] on account of his craft to make them doors and couches and milkpails and boxes'; but it is also clearly set out that he was 'not very skilful as a carpenter' and that he owed his reputation to his son, who magically adjusted his work and corrected his mistakes. One day, for example, the 'King of Jerusalem' called Joseph to him and ordered him to make 'a throne of the measure of the place where I have been used to sit'. Joseph laboured two full years to make this throne, but when he carried it to the palace to install it he found that its depth was two spans shorter than the proper measure; whereat the king was angered and the carpenter, fearful of retribution and regretting his lost years of work, 'passed the night supperless and tasting nothing whatsoever'. But the next morning, when he returned to the palace in fear and trembling, Jesus accompanied him, and said quite simply, 'take thee one side of the throne and I will take the other, to set it right. And when Joseph had done as the Lord Jesus had said, and each had pulled on his own side, the throne was made right and brought to the exact measure of the place.' A curious and ingenious miracle, which in one shape or another is reported in all of the apocryphals which deal with the boyhood of Jesus.

In mediaeval times some thought that Jesus did not confine himself to carpentering, and there was a view that he was articled to a man of law; but this was probably special pleading, and if there was ever an early text which developed this theme it disappeared long ago. Others claimed, with more logic than at first appears, that he was apprenticed to a dyer, and there is a textual basis for this story in the Arabic Gospel, though this has it that he was not specifically apprenticed to the trade, but that on one occasion he played a magical trick on a certain dyer called Salem. In this man's absence he went into his shop, and finding there a pile of cloths waiting their turn to be dyed in the many vats of different colours, he picked them up, and dropped them indiscriminately and together into a vat filled with 'Indian blue', or indigo. It is not surprising that when the dyer returned he was horrified: '. . . Thou hast rendered me dishonourable among all my townsmen, for every one wished for the colour which suited him, but thou hast

91 Jesus is about to pull at the wood and so adjust Joseph's faulty carpentry. From a French manuscript, fifteenth century.

come and ruined all. The Lord Jesus answered, of whatever cloth thou wishest the colour changed, I will change it for thee, and he began at 89 (3) once to take the cloths out of the vessel, each of them dyed to the colour which the dyer desired, until he had drawn them all out'.

This strange story may be a very late addition to the Arabic Gospel, for there seems to be no evidence of any special connection of the Jews with the dyer's trade in the earlier centuries after the destruction of the Temple. But by at least the twelfth century, and even in areas where the Jews were not particularly engaged in trading in cloth, it appears that the art of dying had become something of a national vocation. Benjamin of Tudela, an intrepid traveller who reached Ceylon and returned to Spain by way of Russia and northern Europe, visited Palestine in the year 1170 and found that in the towns only handfuls of his co-religionists remained, almost all of them dyers, and that the two hundred Jewish families remaining in Jerusalem, where they were allowed a quarter of the city *intra muros*, bought each year from their Muslim rulers the exclusive rights to the town's dying trade. In 1231 Frederic II, in his *Lex Augustalis*, gave the Jews the handling of the royal cloth-dying monopoly; and in countries to the north of the Mediterranean special levies on Jews were sometimes called the 'Tincta', the dyer's tax. The association, then, was strong; and while in mediaeval times Jesus was by no means thought of as a young Jewish boy, it seemed not unreasonable to remember the dyer's shop in Nazareth and by extension, and in a not untypical mediaeval thought process, to believe that a Christian Jesus, the poor and the humble, was a 'prentice boy to the dyer's trade.

The child whom we have known is now a youth, and perhaps a young man, and our sources of information on his early life are drying up. We have glimpses of him in a singular work called 'The History of Joseph the Carpenter', which originated in Egypt somewhere between

opposite
92 A complex narrative picture showing the forbears of Jesus and Mary. On the skyline, centre, is Mount Carmel with the chapel of Agabus to the right; and on its slope Esmerentia and the Carmelites are granted the vision in the sky of the Jesus who is to be. The Carmelites explain to her what this portends and—a solitary figure— she returns to her parents' home, the castle of Sephorus (top left). She explains to them what has happened; and in the left-hand room they interview her suitors, of whom Stollanus is the nearest figure. Below, on the left, the marriage of Esmerentia and Stollanus; centre, the birth and bathing of Anne, with Stollanus kneeling at the bedside in prayer; above this, Anne and Joachim are married in a chapel; and their charity to the poor is displayed before the timbered house. Below, on the right, Joachim's offering to the Temple is refused. They are a much older couple than they were on their wedding day, but above, top right, angelic messengers announce to Joachim, in the hills with his flocks, and to Anne in her garden in 'Nazareth' the future motherhood of Anne who will bear Mary, who herself will be the mother of Jesus. Note that the identification of persons at different times and places is sartorial, e.g. Stollanus's red hat and splendid fur-trimmed robe (shown three times), or Joachim's edged cloak which he wears in four scenes from his marriage to the Annunciation in the hills, twenty years later. Flemish, *c.* 1500.

overleaf
93 Esmerentia's eventual marriage with Stollanus. In the background are all her previous husbands, dead or dying under the hand of the demon Asmodeus. By a fifteenth-century Brussels master.

the fourth and the seventh centuries and which gives us at least one major detail of his life at home: 'Justus and Simeon the elder sons of Joseph, having married wives, went away with their families. Both the daughters likewise married and went to their houses. But Judas and James the Less, and the virgin my mother, remained in the house of Joseph. I also continued along with them . . .' Jesus, then, in this account, remains with the family in a considerably reduced household in which Joseph, the protagonist of this story, would have had less mouths to feed. Egypt, and its semi-dependant churches in Ethiopia, were already Marial country, and in these early centuries they were the only parts of the Christian world where Joseph was already the not inconsiderable cult figure which he became in the West almost a thousand years later. This 'History' tells us of certain incidents of his life, and in particular celebrates its end which, in the death-cult fashion of the Egyptians, is set out at great length. Until his extreme old age he laboured, it is said, under no bodily infirmities and 'always displayed a youthful vigour in his affairs, his members remaining whole and free from pain'. But his mortal illness, when it came upon him, was prolonged, painful, and dream-wracked. At the last his family sur-rounded the bed and for a long time Mary massaged his feet, knowing by their increasing coldness that death was near. When the end came, Jesus mourned him: 'Then came into my mind the day he journeyed with me into Egypt, and that great trouble which he endured on my account. Then I wept for his death for a long time, and bent over his body in sorrow'. The mortal remains of the 'good old man' did not decay, the archangels Michael and Gabriel wafted his soul to Heaven; and there was a great keening of the inhabitants of Nazareth and all Galilee.

From this point on, from the death of Joseph as it is recorded in this tertiary source, we know no more of the younger Jesus. No text available to us today and no lost source to which any serious reference has been made in the past gives us a single detail of his young manhood. Clement of Rome, in his Epistle to the Corinthians, of which we have a text which probably antedates all other Christian writings, gives us a remarkable physical description of the Jesus of the years which preceded the Ministry, one which in no way tallies with the handsome

overleaf
94 Top left, the birth of Anne, while in the foreground, Anne as a young girl is introduced to the Carmelites by her parents. By a fifteenth-century Brussels master.

opposite
95 The Virgin and Child with St Jerome and St Sebastian. By Carlo Crivelli (*c.* 1430– *c.* 1495).

96 The Carpenter's Shop, by Arthur Hughes, nineteenth century.

westerner of a later time who degenerates into the images of St Sulpice. But that is part of another story. In this, our own history of the forbears and the early days of Jesus we have come to the end of the tale which began at the marriage of Joachim and Anne, and which has taken us through much uncanonical supposition and much invention; and which, supported by texts of great antiquity and by traditions and folk memories too strong and widespread to be easily denied, has sometimes permitted us to hear, distantly but clearly, from the other side, as it were, of the valley, the accents of truth. Now the life of Jesus passes into the shadows and we do not hear of him again until the great John said of him *He it is, who coming after me is preferred before me, whose shoe's latchet I am not worthy to unloose:* and who on the next day was baptised in the waters of Jordan.

12 The great-grandparents · a postscript

55   The Introduction to this book began with those three central figures of the Holy Family whose characteristics are known to everyone and whose attributes lie at the heart of the Christian religion. As we have progressed, we have added at least some names and some details to the 'Holy Kinship' of blood or marriage which is grouped round this inner and special circle: Mary has been given a well documented mother and father, we know much more of Joseph, and even Jesus' brothers and sisters have emerged somewhat from their biblical shadows. John the Baptist and his parents, who are themselves part of the 'Holy Kinship', have come on the scene more than once and we know far more of their lives than we can learn from the New Testament. The only other character who has had a lasting part to play has been

37   Salome and even she, according to certain traditions, was Mary's second cousin. Extraneous characters like Maia the midwife and

75   Alsamandar Porlac the Egyptian prince, have appeared in their respective places, performed their tasks and vanished from our sight. It remains a restricted family circle; and the apocryphal books, in the proper sense of that term, do not extend it further.

   The genealogical table (page 188) tells another story. It contains the

12 98   names of no less than 37 figures, all of whom are related to one another in various degrees. Joachim and Anne, and Joseph and Mary, united in their respective marriages form the linking figures. Certain names appear twice, reflecting the complexity of Jewish family relationships; the table itself has been built up from many disparate sources, some very far from biblical Palestine; and the whole is an amalgam of personages many of whom we see but indistinctly. Malthan, for example —in that spelling—the ancestor of the left-hand group, is known from ancient Persian texts and he and his descendance appear both in the Bible and in apocryphal works; and among the difficulties of constructing a genealogy of this kind, his name has been a beacon. He is the Matthat of Luke's biblical table of ascendance and the only name among the forbears of Joseph the Carpenter on which Luke and Matthew —who calls him Matthan—agree; and he appears again in the works of Ephraim the Syrian. Yet he himself remains a shadowy figure and

The Holy Kinship

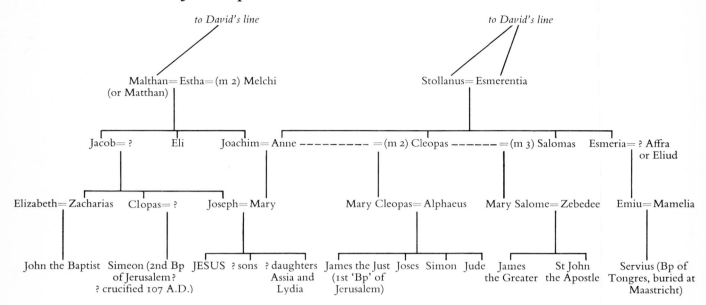

we should dearly like to know more of this man who in so many places and times, and by Christian and non-Christians alike, was remembered, however imperfectly, by name.

The right hand side of the table, on the other hand, presents a picture of a different and an altogether special kind. It is made up, particularly in its senior generations, of personages who are the inventions of a particular area and period and of particular religious groups which were characterised by a devotion to Mary of so ecstatic a kind that it may not unreasonably be termed Mariolotry. Here, we are moving from the apocryphal into a realm of pure fantasy where the wish was father to the thought, and the thought was made flesh. At the heart of the basic story or invention lie Stollanus and Esmerentia: Esmerentia, the ancestress, lived with her wealthy parents at the foot of Mount Carmel, in the castle of Sephorus, a structure so massive that even in the fourteenth century of our own era the traveller de Maundeville was taken to ruins which he was told were those of her palace. She was brought up by her parents in conditions of exemplary piety, and while still a child she had dedicated herself to perpetual virginity. Her days were spent in prayer with the monks of Carmel—'Carmelites' —who had frequent premonitions of an exceptional destiny which awaited her; and on the slopes of the mountain where they congregated they were visited by an angel and granted, in Esmerentia's presence, the vision of a child who was to be born in no long space of time and who was to be the saviour of the world. It was deduced by the watchers that one of their number had been set apart by the will of Heaven to be the ancestor of that child, and that the chosen vessel could not but be Esmerentia, who was the only one of the company who, because of her age, had not yet taken her final vows. She must, they concluded, marry and bear a child.

Accepting this great change in her fortunes and her future, she
72 returned home and told her parents what had passed; and they, deeply impressed by a vision attested to by such respectable witnesses and hoping for a glorious descendance through the person of their daughter, made immediate preparations for the selection of a husband, and for her marriage. Naturally, a crowd of suitors jostled for the hand of this rich and beautiful young woman, and one after another were successful in carrying off the prize. Esmerentia was in fact married no less than six times. But each of her husbands, as they approached the threshold of the bridal chamber on the wedding night, permitted himself to think 'carnal thoughts'; and for this indelicacy, this lack of respect towards that eventual, that sacred progeny which the Carmelites
93 had seen in the sky, each was struck down in his turn and slain by the demon Asmodeus. But the bride's persistance—and indeed that of her suitors—was eventually rewarded: her seventh marriage was to Stollanus, a man noble, rich and of exemplary piety. This time, all— as it seems at first sight—went well, and in due course a daughter was
72 94 born who was given the name of Anne.

We know little of her childhood save that she vowed herself, as her mother had done, to perpetual chastity; and that she also was
94 turned from her purpose by the persistent Carmelites who continually surrounded her with their attentions and who had visions of an extra-ordinary tree with spreading branches and 'suave' fruit, which they identified with her progeny. It was on their advice that she was married to Joachim, that rich and dedicated pillar of the church, which they seem to have forgotten was the Jewish church; and so this Anne who was Emerentia's child from Carmel became identified with the Anne of apocryphal history. The story of their wedded life has been given in Chapter 1, and here we must record its end, and look at the complicated marital history of Anne herself, as it is set out in this remarkable tale. Joachim, it was said, died soon after the dedication of Mary to the Temple and Anne, left alone in her house and longing to replace the child who was no longer with her, became the wife of a man called Cleopas, by whom she also had a daughter whom she again called Mary in order that this child should be a constant reminder of her first-born. Cleopas died in his turn and Anne, who must have been by now well advanced in years, was married once again to one Salomas,

by whom she had yet a third daughter, once again a Mary and generally distinguished from the others by the name Mary Salome; and in late mediaeval and early Renaissance times these three were often taken, in a ripe confusion, for the 'Three Maries' who stood beneath the cross.

To the second Mary, in this scheme of things, was attributed four sons, who are precisely those which the New Testament names as the brothers of Jesus. Here they become his second cousins, which removes the stain of child-bearing from Mary the Virgin. The belief that they stood in this relationship to Jesus is an ancient one, for we find in the early Bridlington Dialogue that the Magister speaks of James the Less, 'who was called the Lord's brother because he was the son of the Saviour's aunt'; which is close enough to our own definition, which comes from quite other sources than those available to the Bridlington author. The third Mary, Mary Salome, this time in full agreement with the New Testament story, married Zebedee and gave him two sons James and John, of which the second is often, and confidently, designated as that shadowy figure John the Evangelist. This complex descendance of Anne is set out in a verse of a German monastic hymn of the early fifteenth century which accords perfectly with the Carmelite premonitions:

98

Anna radix uberrima,	O Anna, fecund stem!
Arbor te salutifera.	O salutary tree!
Virgas producens triplices,	Thrusting out your triple branches
Septimus onusta fructas.	Seven times laden with their fruit.

The three Maries are the three branches, and their sons, from Jesus himself onwards, are the seven fruit of this monkish canticle.

There remains the last group, descended from Esmeria the second daughter of Esmerentia. Of Esmeria and her son and grandson we know almost nothing, though they duly appear, suitably labelled with their respective names, in gatherings of the Holy Kinship. And sometimes, in more arboreal genealogies similar to Jesse trees we find them peeping out at us from among the branches. But with the last of the line, Servatus, we come out into the full light of day, and the outline of his story—which is certainly a late one, and independant of the main theme—deserves the telling. As a young man Servatus, or Servius, went to Rome where St Peter, deeply impressed by his piety, made him the ultimate gift: a duplicate set—though only in silver—of the Keys of Heaven. Four hundred years later, in one of those leaps

98

97 Esmerentia and the Carmelite monks receive the vision of the future Jesus; from an altarpiece by Bernard van Orley (*c.* 1492–*c.* 1541).

throught time which, with his lack of historical definition, did not in any way disconcert mediaeval man, Attila and his Huns came upon Servius asleep in a field, his eyes shaded from the sun by the hovering wings of an eagle; and the sight of this marvel, and the sermon which he took the opportunity of preaching when he awoke, were sufficient to convert the savage host to the true faith. His life was one of active piety, and he became the scourge of thieving boys and the benefactor and eventually a patron of vintners and orchard keepers. At an ill-defined date he became the Bishop of Tongres in the Mosan country, where the enraged peasantry—we do not know why—beat him to death with their sabots, which became his attributes; so that if one sees a representation of a mitred bishop with three little sabots lying at his feet, that is he. As St Servius he was buried in the cathedral of Maastricht, where you can see his tomb today, where a section of the town bears his name, and where he is honoured—as he is at Cologne and Liege, as St Servais—with fitting ceremony at his annual festival.

With Servatus, who can serve as a symbol of a manner of thought, we come to the end of the strange story of Esmerentia and her descendance: which is essentially a tale of women to whom are linked a whole generation of Apostles and biblical figures who give a special sanctity to the 'Holy Kinship' which surrounds the central characters of Mary and Jesus and a special lustre to Esmerentia and her Carmelite-directed

98 A full gathering of the Holy Kinship: God himself and the Holy Spirit are in the centre, top, and all the family is present, down to little Servatus on his mother's knee, bottom left. Jesus is making his 'First Steps' between his mother and grandmother; and to help those who could not read the phylacteries or who were uncertain of the story, the husbands standing above are pointing to or looking at their wives seated below. The scene was painted in the Low Countries in 1562.

inspirations. Clearly defined apocryphal personages—Anne and Joachim—have been linked in with the story to give it a more persuasive ring of truth; for with the apocryphal evidence before us it is not difficult for us to believe even today that Anne was an historical character as real, say, as Elizabeth in Luke. Had the contrary been true it would have been necessary, as we shall see, to invent her in order to provide Mary with a mother of a special kind and of a special type of sanctity. Anne's *raison d'être* was to be that mother just as, by extension, Esmerentia was invented to fill a similar role for Anne herself.

For invented she was. The story of Anne's birth at Safir or Sefor or Sephorus was an old one; and if a traveller like de Maundeville could actually visit that stronghold some fourteen centuries later, that was the business of the Palestine of the time which seldom let slip the opportunity to provide attractions for the pious tourist. But the person of her mother Esmerentia was specifically called into existence, at a special time and in a special and essentially sombre climate of religiosity and ecstatic Marialism. It was said that her story and that of her marriage and descendance were revealed in repeated celestial visions to a young nun who became St Colette, and who early in the fourteenth century reintroduced rigorous rules to the order of the Poor Clares. This may have been so; the time was in any case ripening for necessary extension to Mary's forbears in the female line.

By the end of the century, unquestioning faith in the sanctity and efficacy of the church as the transmitting vessel for received truth was giving way, in certain quarters, to doubt; and doubt, by its existence, created an answering and intense religious fervour. This found its deepest expression in Northern France, the Low Countries and the valley of the Rhine, and in particular in the many Carmelite houses which were in the area. The Carmelites of the time believed that their order had its origins in remote antiquity: Mount Carmel, from which they took their name, had been a peculiarly sacred spot ever since that day when Elijah's servant, from its summit, had seen the *little cloud out of the sea, like a man's hand*, and it was held that solitaries and even regulars of the order had lived on its slopes since long before the time of Jesus—*vide* Esmerentia's companions in prayer—and that Agabus, Mary's earliest suitor, had built on its summit the first chapel, a Carmelite chapel, ever to be dedicated to her. It was said that here, and for this chapel, St Luke had painted his portrait of the Virgin with which the Carmelites of a later day, when the picture had darkened with age, had fled to Italy at the time of the Muslim conquests, where it became known as 'La Bruna', 'en raison de la teinte de sa carnation': her 'complexion'. Something of the kind happened. Many copies of a picture were made. One was in Constantinople, another in Milan; and

99 The Black Virgin of Montserrat. Abadia de Montserrat, Spain.

99 it is tempting to speculate that perhaps there, in those troubled times, lies the distant origin of the 'Black Virgin' statues which are to be found in the cathedral at Chartres, for instance, or at Montserrat, and in so many of the churches of Christendom.

Under the tolerant Saracens, Carmel became again a haunt of Christian hermits; and when the Carmelite Order was actually founded in Palestine by St Bertholdus in the year 1154, some of these anchorites may have associated themselves with it and given the order an early lustre of antiquity. Only thirty years later Phocas the Greek visited the place and found 'Holy men . . . leading solitary lives on Mount Carmel . . . where in little honeycomb cells these bees of the Lord lay up spiritual honey'; and he knew of a tradition that their predecessors had been there from ancient times.

It is not surprising, then, that the Carmelites, who believed implicitly in these solid and enviable associations of their order not only with the Holy Land but with the earthly life of the Virgin herself, should, in a Marial age, have become the most ardent of Marialists. They created a dialectic and defended their position against the Schoolmen; and during the fifteenth century, in response to the dangerous religious speculation of the times, these preoccupations intensified to a marvellous degree. Their ardent Marialism centred, more than ever before, around the concept of Mary's unsullied virginity and its primordial role in the doctrine of redemption from original sin. This passionate theology and the burning desire which accompanied it to affirm the direct association of their order with the Mother of God, led to the creation of Esmerentia, the capture of Anne and hence the creation of Carmelite forbears for, and a consequent Carmelite influence over, a majority of the Apostles; and even, of course, over Mary herself, and Jesus.

We must look at the position to which this led: Mary's majestic distinction was that she was not only the mother of God, but the bride of God, who had borne His son and who alone among women had been a virgin mother; and this her virginity was the hope for the world's salvation. Long ago, Adam and Eve, for their sin of disobedience to Jehovah in their eating of the forbidden fruit—which is called an apple—and in their resulting carnal knowledge of each other when their eyes were opened, had lost their innocence, and their garden of delights. They had been condemned to perpetuate their 'original' sin through the physical procreation of children, and they of their children's children, for evermore. Each succeeding generation inherited the sin of their first ancestors and inherited their condemnation, so that through all past time they had known no other lot than to gain their bread by the sweat of their brow and to eat that bread in sorrow. But now through Mary the Sacred Vessel, the mother and the virgin, Jesus had been conceived of the Godhead, the carnal, the earthly chain of generation was broken, and the first innocence of God's creation was seen again in the person of the Son of God who had descended on earth to show mankind the way to forgiveness and a new salvation. Through his divine conception and by his birth among men the Satanic apple, the forbidden fruit, had lost its power. This triumph over the powers of evil is symbolically, and repeatedly, demonstrated in mediaeval artifacts of the mother and child in which we see Mary handing the apple, the apple of the tree of life, to her son. Jesus, accepting it, is the recreated Adam in the state of original grace; and Mary, repeating the gesture which had been made in the first of gardens, is again the unsullied Eve. Together, they are acting out the ancient scene and exorcising the ancient sin: clearing the way, as they do so, for the even more complex theology of the redemption of mankind through the ultimate sacrifice of Jesus.

95 The Crivelli *conversazione* which is here reproduced is a striking presentation of these concepts. Dating from 1494, the picture is executed with all the brilliance and technical mastery of the Renaissance; yet it is imbued with the sombre emotions and the sombre theology which belong more properly to late mediaeval times. The picture allows the hope of Grace; but it is concerned with death: and it demonstrates not a moment in time, but the future of its characters, of which all of them are aware. Mary has given her son the apple of original sin and she fixes her regard upon him with sadness and resignation, conscious of the event to come which will be the greatest of her seven sorrows. St Sebastian is melancholy, withdrawn, fingering the symbolic arrow of his martyrdom. St Jerome is old, his work is done. He carries his writings in his hand, and a model of the basilica in Bethlehem which will be his tomb; and as he looks across with sorrow at one who is to die so young, he points his way to salvation. Jesus himself, from the beginning all-seeing and all-knowing, fixes his melancholy gaze on the church which he will found and inspire by his crucifixion and his resurrection. No single element of the picture is without meaning: the fruit and the flowers which surround the throne, the swallow and the gherkin and the hangings, symbolically recall the whole theology of the church. Even here, on the threshold of the sixteenth century, all is still symbol, all is divine, and the tangible exists but to demonstrate its inner significance and its hidden verities. 'Paintings', indeed, 'be
2 but naked letters for the clerk to reden the truth'.

Of the two supporting figures, St Sebastian is the Church Militant, St Jerome is the Church Contemplative. Jesus is their founder, the hope of the world. But even he is shown in an awkward position, offset on his mother's knee. She, Mary the Virgin, the Ineffable, is the central character and she dominates the picture. Here is the Queen of Heaven, a far cry from the little Jewish girl who came out of the biblical shadows to be the bride of Joseph. That Mary had been an anonymous, a human and imperfect woman, an imperfect vessel for a complex and intricate devotion. In the canon, her involvement in the act of redemption came with, and by, the heavenly conception and the consequent virgin birth of Jesus; and by those events alone. Until that time she was by definition as unregenerated, as filled with original sin, as Joseph himself, or as any other man or woman in Judea. In late mediaeval times, when Mary had been clothed in her mantle as the Ineffable and Heavenly Queen, this situation was intolerable. In her special and unique case it was perfectly necessary to retrogress by at least a generation the cleansing and redemptive force which she represented and to free the Virgin herself, from the moment of her own conception, from any stain.

Such a concept was not easy to formulate or to systematise theologically, and biblical sources, as we have seen, gave no help. In the civilised and Orthodox lands of Byzantium, whose stability and Levantine traditions allowed the luxury of contemplative mysticism at a far earlier date than in the West, Mary had been already established by the seventh century as 'Theotokos' the God-bearer who was required, by definition to be sinless; and from that time we begin to find in the East artifacts which tell the tale of Joachim and Anne whose parenthood, arising solely from the 'Kiss at the Golden Gate', accorded the special
23 circumstances to Mary's birth which were required to mark it out from that of the rest of mankind. As we have seen in Chapter 1, the idea took long, very long, to penetrate the western church, though from the ninth century we begin to find representations of Anne's story in areas particularly subject to Byzantine influence. And when the tale was brought back, as if it had been a *trouvaille,* by the first of the returning crusaders, it was welcomed in some circles as warmly as it was disputed on the grounds of probability, and of traditional theology, by most of the Schoolmen, with St Bernard at their head. But the idea gained ground and before 1300 Giotto, almost certainly following an established tradition, was celebrating the miracle of Mary's birth on the walls of the Arena chapel in Padua; and the church establishment, accepting what it could not, and in the end would not wish to stifle, began to give the subject a sanction which eventually became so wholehearted that within a century of Giotto's time a declared belief in the absolute sinlessness of Mary from the moment of her conception became, for example, a requirement for admission to the universities of France and Italy.

In establishing this sinlessness, the story of Anne and Joachim struck a correct theological and mystical balance. If the birth of Mary had been brought about by the direct intervention of the Divine, Anne, as a second virgin mother, would have become the rival of her daughter.
17 But she and Joachim had lived a normal, if childless life for twenty years; and then, in a moment of despair and separation which heightened the drama, Divine machinery had been set in motion which established
14 22 what were, in effect, Annunciations of a less exalted class than that
30 which was to be made to their daughter. The couple were reunited and Mary's conception was brought about, not by any carnal act, but by that chaste kiss at the Golden Gate. Between this kiss, and the birth of her child, Anne lived in chastity. The circumstances, then, of Mary's birth were such that they freed her as entirely from the sin of Adam, the

100 Anne enthroned in majesty, with her daughter and grandson. Both she and the donatrix are Carmelites; and it is *Anne* who offers the forbidden fruit of Eden to the infant Jesus, the Redeemer. She has usurped her daughter's place; here it is she who is the new Eve and she who acts out the ancient gesture. Spanish, fifteenth century.

original sin, as was possible without destroying the unique character of the birth of her own son Jesus, whom Mary was to conceive through the direct, the physical intervention of the Divine.

Mary then obtained this additional, this signal elevation, which none welcomed more than the Carmelites of the Rhine and the Low Countries. But by implication Anne herself was lifted to the highest spheres of the Christian hierarchy and she became an object of exceptional devotion to these Regulars, and to many of the Seculars and laity who were influenced, not only by the Carmelites themselves, but by the general character of the dark and orgulous devotions of the fifteenth century. It was a time for ecstasy: and the need was felt for the adoration of Anne to be directed towards her as a being who herself had been brought sinless into the world. It was not easy to achieve this end. For the birth of Mary herself a suitable story had been to hand and had required only to be formalised. But Anne's own parentage was unknown, and it was necessary to establish one.

The visions of Colette — let us say — created an answer which was agreeable to the temper of the time, and more agreeable still as the fourteenth century merged into the fifteenth. They provided an Esmerentia of exceptional piety who had the additional advantage of elevating and distinguishing the Order by her daily devotions, at that distant time, with the Carmelites on Carmel. Esmerentia required a Stollanus for her protection, together with the exceptional marital circumstances which were provided by the repeated bridegrooms who lost no less than life itself to the Devil for their carnal thoughts. Stollanus himself, as was proper, remained a shadowy figure and the actual circumstances of the conception of Anne were left imprecise. But 'to God', it was said, 'all things are possible', and the ardent and innocent Regulars of the Carmelites would have been satisfied with the absence of carnality in her eventual consort and certain that the first substance of that mother of Mary whom they contemplated with fervent adoration would have been brought into the world by a divine, if mysterious, intervention: an intervention which prepared the way for that mystic descendance to Mary the perpetual Annunciatrix in perpetual communion with God, of whose essence, six hundred years ago, de Coincy sang:

> *Elle est la flor, elle est la rose,*
> *En cui reside, en cui repose,*
> *Jour et nuict, Saint Esperiz.*

Bibliography

There is no complete English text of the known apocryphal texts associated with the New Testament. A selection may be found in *The Apocryphal New Testament* of M. R. James (Oxford University Press, 1924, reprinted 1972) which gives the Protevangelium in full together with a version of the Gospel of Thomas and notes on other 'Infancy' material. The standard work on the subject, with full historical and critical apparatus, is the *Neutestamentliche Apocryphen* (1959) of Edgar Hennecke, which has been translated by R. McL. Wilson and others (2 vols.: Lutterworth Press, U.K., and Westminster Press, U.S.A.), but this is sparing in texts. The fullest rendering of works concerned with the Infancy is B. Harris Cowper's *Apocryphal Gospels* (David Nutt, 1897), but this is almost unobtainable today.

We are not much better served in the study of mediaeval artifacts related to the apocryphal events. Tucked away in the *Mémoires* of the Académie Royale de Belgique, XI/3/3b, is a doctoral thesis, 'l'Enfance de la Vierge', by Jacqueline Lafontaine-Desonges, which matches artifacts to the story of the childhood of Mary; and there are two far more ambitious works, both called *Ikonographie der Kristlichen Kunst*, by Karl Künstle (2 vols., 1926) and Gertrud Schiller (1966). But both—and the Schiller in particular—have evangelical terms of reference. The six-volume work of Louis Réau, *l'Iconographie de l'Art Chrétien*, owes something to the iconographic work of Emile Mâle and is a listing of artifacts related to the entire biblical narrative from Genesis to Revelation, and to the lives of the saints, together with excursions into the apocryphal field. Then there is the *Drei Heiligen Königen in Litteratur und Kunst*, by Edgar Kehrer (Leipzig, 1906, 2 vols.). Almost twenty years after this date, Bernard Berenson, in his introduction to the *Speculum Humanae Salvationis*, regretted that this 'exemplary enquiry' was the only full-scale study of the art and letters relating to any of the set pieces of the Christian or apocryphal story; and fifty years later still, the position is unchanged.

The offering of apocryphal texts and apocryphal iconography is meagre. But this book has been in part, and insofar as this was in any way possible within so small a compass, an examination of the mediaeval conditions and cast of thought which permitted apocryphal material to flourish. For further reading in this vast field the author can only put forward, with great temerity, the names of those who have been his unseen companions for many years: thus among the exotics, there is the Koran, in George Sale's translation and with his Introductory Discourse; and the translations from the Ethiopic, Coptic and Syriac of Wallis Budge. Among the older historians of mediaeval matters, Gibbon stands alone; but Hallam may have been unjustly neglected. G. G. Coulton, that inspired magpie, did most to change the nineteenth century conception of mediaeval history to that of the twentieth and even influenced that great repository of information, the *Cambridge Mediaeval History*.

Among the moderns: for the rural and social background to the whole of mediaeval life, Marc Bloch stands first. For its art, E. Panofsky, D. Talbot Rice, Joan Evans, T. S. R. Boase, among many others. For its economics, M. M. Postan, Henri Pirenne, Eileen Power, G. Ostrogorsky. For the Universities, Rashdall is still unsurpassed; and for the Crusades, Steven Runciman; for philosophy, Etienne Gilson, and for heresy, W. L. Wakefield and A. P. Evans. For pilgrimages, the series of the Palestine Pilgrims Text Society, and for late mediaeval Carmelite matters, there are the works of de Tervarent; the *Speculum Carmelitorum*; and Bostius of Ghent. For general history the choice is an especially invidious one, but J. Huizinga, Ernest Powicke, Louis Halphen, Jacques Le Goff and R. W. Southern cover between them a wide spectrum of views. And for mediaeval texts themselves there is the remarkable and constantly growing series edited by the Early English Text Society (Oxford University Press); and Nelson's Mediaeval Classics, where these are still available, together with Caxton's translation of the Golden Legend. For the daily background of biblical and apocryphal times these is Hugh Shonfield. For theology in general one might dare to cite from the great mass of traditionalists the name of Bishop Lightfoot of Durham; and then there are the more recent Christian demystifyers of various persuasions headed by Bonhoeffer, Bultmann and Tillich.

Finally, we have seen that there is little published work on the direct relationship of artifacts to the apocrypha: but a liberal education in schematic iconography can be obtained under elegant and precise guidance in the Photographic Library of the Warburg Institute in London. And no book of this kind could be complete without the name of Constantin von Tischendorf, that craggy giant who in the middle decades of the last century discovered and recognised, often in the remotest corners of Christendom, an astonishing wealth of early Christian writings. Biblical and apocryphal exegesis owe more to him than to any other man and those of us who are sometimes concerned with these disciplines look about us in gratitude from the shelter of his vast and ill-buttoned cloak.

All biblical quotations in this work are printed in italics, and are taken from the Authorised Version of King James I.

Picture Acknowledgements

Permission to reproduce photographs has kindly been given by the following (the picture numbers in italics refer to colour illustrations).

Abadia de Montserrat, Spain: 99. Copyright A. C. L. Brussels, photograph supplied by Thames and Hudson, London: 30. Alinari, Florence: 14. Alte Pinakothek, Munich/Scala, Florence: *23*. Badische Landesbibliothek, Karlsruhe: *53*. Bodleian Library, Oxford: *15*, 35, 46, 60, *72*, *73*, *76*, *77*, *80*, 83, *89*, 91. The President and Fellows of Corpus Christi College, Oxford: *87*. Boymans van Beuningen Museum, Rotterdam: 29. British Library Board: *70*, *78*, *79*, 82. British Library Board, photograph supplied by the Courtauld Institute of Art, London University: 65, 74, 84, 85. British Library Board, photograph supplied by the E. P. Group of Companies: 90. Cappella del Cimitero, Monterchi/Alinari, Florence: 36. Collection Vaunxheim, Paris: 75. Courtauld Institute of Art, London University: 40, 52 (Professor L. Gowing Collection), 58, *64* (Lee Collection). Fürstlich Hohenzollernsches Museum, Sigmaringen, photographs by Foto Nolting: 12, 98. Galleria degli Uffizi, Florence/Scala, Florence: *47*. Ivan W. Green: *55*. Sonia Halliday Photographs: *8*, *9*, *16*, *24*, *25*, *28*, *33*, *41*, *42*, *43*, *48*, *49*, *56*, *71*, 88. Sonia Halliday Photographs, photograph by F. H. C. Birch: *10*. Historisches Museum, Frankfurt a.M.: *93*, *94*. Bob Jones University Collection, Greenville, South Carolina: *50*.

Kunsthalle, Hamburg: 1, 2, 69. Kunstmuseum, Basle: 57. Lautenbach-im-Renchtal, Schwarzwald, Germany: 19. Mansell Collection, London: 5. Mikuszowice Church, Poland: 68. Musée de Dijon/Bulloz, Paris: *44*. Musée St Sauveur, Bruges: *92*. Musées de la ville de Strasbourg: 61. Musées Royaux des Beaux-Arts de Belgique, photograph copyright A. C. L. Brussels: 97. Museo Arqueologica, Valladolid: 100. By permission of Ministerio da Educacão e Cultura, in the collection of Museo Nacional de Arte Antiga, Lisbon: *54*. Narodni Museum, Prague, photograph by Antonin Blaha: 11. National Gallery, London: 4, *63*, 95. National Gallery of Victoria, Australia, Felton Bequest 1922: *62*. Österreichische Galerie, Vienna, photograph by Fotostudio Otto: *31*. Photographische Gesellschaft, Berlin: 20. Oscar Poss: 67. Prado, Madrid: 59. John Rylands University Library, Manchester: 6. Scala, Florence: *7*, *17*, *18*, *22*, *26*, *32*. Ronald Sheridan: 37. Sotheby & Co, London: 21. Spedale degl Innocenti, Florence/Brogi: 27. Städelsches Kunstinstitut, Frankfurt a.M.: 39. Staatl. Graphische Sammlung, Munich: 45. Temple Gallery, London: 38. Tiroler Landesmuseum Ferdinandeum, Austria, photograph by A. Demanega: *86*. Vatican Apostolik Library, Rome: 66. Victoria and Albert Museum, London, Crown copyright: 34, 81. Warburg Institute, London University: 3. M. H. de Young Memorial Museum, San Francisco, gift of Samuel H. Kress Foundation: 51.

Endpaper: Map of the Holy Land, *c.* 1625. Collection Sydney Franklin Esq., London.

Index